1,000 Example Sentences to Help You 'Show' Not 'Tell' in Writing

Covers 50 Emotions to Help You Create Impact!

The ultimate secret weapon for anyone wanting to ACE their writing test!

Exam Success

Copyright & Disclaimer

Dedication

This book is dedicated to all the children and
adults who make an effort to develop their writing skills.
I hope this book is helpful to you and makes it easier for you
to write with impact.
Crafting a story takes patience and time.
Kudos to you, the storyteller.

Table of Contents

CHAPTER ONE

Introduction - The Easy Way to 'Show'

'Showing' your writing was hard, now it's easy

Writing a narrative should be quite simple, right?

Well... it depends on what kind of narrative you want.

Writing an *average* story is **easy**—you just come up with a story and tell the story.

But, writing an A+ scoring, top-notch story is *really* **hard**.

What separates the A+ story from the average one?

The magic ingredient is 'showing'.

'Showing' the story is about creating a 'feeling' - making the story memorable and making people feel an emotion when they read it.

When someone tells you a story, it's as if you were hearing a news report—there is little emotion and you're told what happens.

'Showing' brings the story to life, just as if you were watching a movie, and people not only imagine your story, they see it visually in their mind's eye. Through your story, they are transported into another world.

'Showing' makes your story memorable. And this is what gets you the marks (if you're doing an exam) or your reader's attention!

This book was created because 'showing' is hard.

There are so many emotions that you can show and showing requires you to be very selective with the words you include.

Use the wrong word and your 'showing' sentence loses its impact, or worse, creates confusion.

Additionally, there are certain situations or symbols that can represent specific emotions.

For example, you wouldn't use an old rickety chair when trying to convey an emotion of confidence or when someone is extremely happy. Instead, an old rickety chair would be a perfect symbol to show the feelings of abandonment, loneliness and pity.

Knowing what symbols and situations to use in 'showing' certain emotions helps take your writing to the next level.

This book was created to help your writing go from average to **incredible**.

'Showing' in fiction writing is what boosts your written expression score to an A+, but many students and writers don't do it or don't know how to do it. This is because the process of 'showing' your writing is **hard**.

You have to come up with a situation, then select the right words and finally put it together nicely.

This book helps to make the work of 'showing' easier for you with 1,000 sample sentences to 'show' your story.

This book *is* your secret-weapon so that when you're writing, you'll be able to 'show' your story easily and with incredible impact.

How to use this book - Start 'Showing' in 4 Steps!

You can use this book to start writing amazing 'showing' stories, in just 4 simple and easy steps:

1. *Write your story.*

2. *Underline a few sentences in each paragraph of your story that 'tell'.* Telling sentences are often short sentences that tell you what happened. Examples of telling sentences are: 'I was sad that day' or 'I was happy that I won'. Remember, you don't want to underline all telling sentences in your paragraph because you want to keep a balance of 'showing' sentences and 'telling' sentences. When every sentence in a paragraph is a 'showing' sentence, a writing piece can appear 'overdecorated' to the reader. Only underline a few sentences that 'tell' so that you can change them to 'show' the story.

3. *Select a replacement sentence in the book that best suits your needs.* This book outlines 50 emotions or states of being and this has been grouped in larger areas like 'happiness' and 'sadness'. Go through the table of contents to find out which of these areas best suit and then select your replacement 'showing' sentence.

4. *Modify the replacement sentence and insert it where the original 'telling' sentence was.* This part is really important. When you have selected your sentence, it is important to modify it so that it will fit your story. Do not use the replacement sentence word for word because your story will likely appear mismatched.

Let's see this in action.

This is an edited paragraph taken from examsuccess.com.au.

> *I didn't even notice my mother coming into my room. She comforted me and told me there was going to be another competition! I was so excited. I decided that I was going to put in my best effort and win the contest once and for all.*

Let's do Steps 2 to 4.

Step 2: Underline a few telling sentences.

> *I didn't even notice my mother coming into my room.* <u>*She comforted me and told me there was going to be another competition!*</u> <u>*I was so excited.*</u> *I decided that I was going to put in my best effort and win the contest once and for all.*

Step 3: Select a replacement sentence in the book that best suits your needs.

Sentence (original)	Selected sentence (showing)
She comforted me and told me there was going to be another competition!	Clare grinned and raised an eyebrow, glad to see that her campaign was gaining supporters. *This sentence was taken from the area of "hopefulness".*
I was so excited.	Jenna's eyes widened and her jaw dropped halfway to the floor. *This sentence was taken from the area of "ecstasy".*

Step 4: Modify the replacement sentence and insert it where the original 'telling' sentence was.

Sentence (original)	Selected sentence (showing)	New sentence
She comforted me and told me there was going to be another competition!	Clare grinned and raised an eyebrow, glad to see that her campaign was gaining supporters.	She grinned and raised an eyebrow—there was going to be another competition after all!
I was so excited.	Jenna's eyes widened and her jaw dropped halfway to the floor.	My eyes widened and my jaw dropped halfway to the floor.

Now that we have our new sentences, let's put these back into our paragraph and compare both paragraphs.

Paragraph (original)	Selected sentence (showing)
I didn't even notice my mother coming into my room. <u>She comforted me and told me there was going to be another competition! I was so excited.</u> I decided that I was going to put in my best effort and win the contest once and for all.	I didn't even notice my mother coming into my room. <u>She grinned and raised an eyebrow—there was going to be another competition after all! My eyes widened and my jaw dropped halfway to the floor.</u> I decided that I was going to put in my best effort and win the contest once and for all.

You'll see that the original paragraph was shorter and tells the reader what happens. The second paragraph shows excitement.

Now... go forth and write amazing showing sentences—the kind that enhances your writing and helps you get top writing scores!

Finding Sentences

This book is set up in a way where you can find 'showing' sentences based on a feeling or emotion that you are trying to create in your writing piece.

The book is set up in the following way:

- **Emotion & Perception**—there are 10 major areas in this book so that you can better pinpoint what you need. These areas are arranged in alphabetical order and are: anger, anticipation, disgust, fear, happiness, mistrust, pride, sadness, surprise and emotion perception.

- **Individual Feeling** —Within each of the 10 major areas, there are a number of feelings that show different levels of intensity for that particular area. For example, ecstatic and amusement all fall under "happiness" even though one is a strong form of happiness and the other, a mild form.

- **Surroundings, Appearance and Action**—You'll further be able to find the exact sentence you're after by looking under 'surroundings', 'appearance' or 'action'. For example, you may want to show your reader that someone is conceited by how they look, that is, through their appearance. You may want to show depression through the surroundings and you may want to show playfulness through someone's actions.

How to improve your writing before your exam

You won't have this book with you at the exam (unless you sneak it in somehow—and I wouldn't recommend doing that!), so how can you improve your writing before your exam?

One word—**practice**.

After you write your essay, complete steps 2 to 4 in *How to use this book* multiple times.

Try it with different sentences and see what kind of impact it creates.

By doing this repeatedly, you're going to build up your arsenal of 'showing' sentences that you'll be able to use and change up for your writing pieces.

Let's get started on each of the emotions, feelings and showing sentences.

CHAPTER TWO

Anger

We've all felt angry and the feeling is part of being human.

Anger is one of those basic feelings that come out even when we're very young. It could be when someone has borrowed your toy and not given it back on time.

People can get angry for important reasons but there are times when people can get angry over petty things. Anger, although a powerful emotion, can be very destructive to the person feeling the anger.

In this chapter, you're going to see how you can express, in words, different levels and types of anger for the characters in your story.

Contempt

One type of anger that can be a very powerful weapon in any writer's arsenal is contempt.

Contempt is the feeling that a person, place, or thing is totally worthless, beneath any sort of consideration, and/or worthy of scorn. If one character feels contempt for another, it shows that they don't care about their problems, and just wish that they would go away.

All stories focus on the main character's attempts to overcome obstacles, and contempt is a great way to make that struggle more complex and interesting; if a main character simply gets everything that he or she needs without any difficulties, their story would be very short and incredibly boring!

Instead, writers make sure that their characters meet people who hold them in contempt: people who just don't like them, and want to see them fail to achieve their goals.

Here are some examples of ways that you can show contempt in your stories.

Surroundings

1. When he first stepped out of the subway station, he knew that the city didn't care whether he lived or died. Businessmen shoved him towards the curb, unwilling to let some hayseed make them late for their meetings, police officers hassled him for loitering but wouldn't give him directions—even the pigeons seemed to sneer at him, as if to say, "Go back to where you came from!"

2. She sat in the waiting room of the modeling agency, surrounded by posters of beautiful people rolling their eyes and laughing at the thought that she could be anything like them.

3. When he walked into the lunch room, it seemed like all of the other kids spread out their books and trays a little further around them, daring him to ask if the seats next to them were open.

4. The dentist's office was a torture chamber, filled with sharp knives and picks that couldn't wait to make her gums bleed.

5. He was a lone genius in a sea of imbeciles; the other cashiers wouldn't even understand the essays he wrote in middle school.

6. She couldn't believe that the casting director picked Lucille to be her stunt double. She looked like her grandmother, with varicose veins and crows' feet that jumped out at her, even across the parking lot.

7. He wanted the ground to open up beneath the parking inspector and swallow him, dragging him back down to Hell, where he belonged.

Appearance

8. He looked at the teacher like she was something unidentified and sticky, coating the bottom of his shoe.

9. She pursed her lips, as if she needed to remind her mouth to remain closed to prevent obscenities from slipping through the cracks.

10. He hardened his gaze in an effort to set the man on fire telekinetically.

11. She raised an eyebrow at the question, but decided that she was above answering it.

12. Her smile was kind, but her dead eyes told the whole story: she'd rather be anywhere else in the world than standing here with her sister.

13. He turned up his nose and recommended the less expensive shoe store across the street with a smirk.

Actions

14. She tripped and skinned her knee, scattering her books across the pavement. A passer-by looked like he was about to bend over and help her, but he only kicked her biology textbook into the dirt with a grin.

15. He pushed past, deliberately ramming his shoulder into him hard enough to spin him half around.

16. She held out his receipt, then yanked it away from him when he tried to grab it.

17. "Thank you," I said. He just blinked and walked away.

18. She bought him a box of chocolate-covered almonds, knowing full well that he was allergic to them.

19. Everyone was clapping after John's breakdancing routine, except Ben, who leaned against a pillar the whole time with his arms crossed.

20. When she told him about the accident, he doubled over laughing.

Fury

When a character is furious, they can lose control of their emotions, their civility, and even their bodies.

They may lash out at other characters physically or emotionally, or strain to keep themselves from doing so. Truly capturing fury on the page can be a challenge, but if you can manage to do it, you can create incredibly dramatic and evocative scenes.

The ultimate display of fury is physical violence. When furious, an otherwise peaceful character may snap and hit another character, which will always result in surprise and interest from the audience.

Below, you'll find some examples of ways to use fury in your own work.

Surroundings

21. Suddenly the room felt like it was one hundred degrees and humid.

22. The room started to black out at the edges, leaving only a tiny pinprick of hate in the middle.

23. She swore that every crack in the sidewalk was put there to remind her of what her stepmother had done.

24. The door was jammed, proving that the universe wanted him to fail. He ripped it open, almost pulling it off its hinges.

25. All around her, children were laughing and playing. She wanted to bend down and tell them that Santa Claus wasn't real, that their friends would betray them and their parents were liars.

26. He must have looked crazy; as he stormed down the sidewalk, the crowd parted to let him through, afraid to become the object of his rage.

27. As if on cue, the clouds burst and lightning flashed on all sides, illuminating her bloodthirsty stare.

Appearance

28. His eyes looked like burning embers, and his teeth were as sharp as fangs.

29. The corner of her mouth twitched so violently that it looked like her jaw might snap.

30. Tears clouded his vision, but he could still see his father standing there, the man who had taken everything away from him.

31. She looked eerily calm, but the lack of blinking gave her away.

32. He bared his teeth like a wild animal.

33. She knitted her brow and scrunched up her nose, as if she could smell the evil in front of her.

Actions

34. He lunged forward and grabbed the killer by his throat.

35. She swung her purse over her head; it connected with the thief's skull with a sickening thwack.

36. He balled his hands into fists. Later on, he'd realize that his nails had cut into his palms, leaving crimson crescents indented in his skin.

37. She read the letter again, then shredded it into confetti over the toilet.

38. He screamed like a slighted child, but it didn't make him feel any better.

39. She weaved in and out of traffic, swinging into the oncoming lane when she couldn't find an opening.

40. The man turned and ran, but he sprinted after him and tackled him to the ground.

Irritation

Irritation is a mild form of anger, characterized by annoyance and impatience.

When a character is irritated, he or she might say rude things that they wouldn't have said on a normal day, or snap at people that might just be trying to help them.

Irritation can be particularly useful for raising the stakes in an otherwise simple or boring situation, making things more interesting or complicated.

A little bit of irritation can go a long way in your stories. Irritated characters can insult others or refuse to do things out of spite, adding drama to otherwise nondramatic scenes.

This irritation can be justified—i.e. the reader would be irritated if they were put in the same situation—or unjustified, which can serve to increase or reduce character sympathy, respectively. Either way, it is bound to make things more interesting and enjoyable for the audience.

Here are some examples of ways to use irritation in your own work.

Surroundings

41. Nothing was going right for her today. Even the cellophane that contained her potato crisps refused to tear open.

42. Of course he chose the longest line in the grocery store, with the woman in front of him leafing through expired coupons and trying to pay with change.

43. She felt like her neighbors staked their signs in the direction of her yard on purpose; they wanted her to leave.

44. He'd worked as a bank teller for twenty years, so he knew that the transaction should only have taken two minutes. The chump behind the desk just wanted to make his life a little more difficult.

45. Everywhere she walked, flocks of tourists would stop short in the middle of her path, deciding that the hardware store window displays were the perfect background for their selfies.

46. He parked in a different spot every morning, but the pigeons just followed his car, aiming their poop at his windshield.

47. She spent months searching for the perfect dress, but when she wore it to the party, no fewer than three pretty girls chose the same one. They must have consulted with each other the night before, conspiring to make her look frumpy by comparison.

Appearance

48. He rolled his eyes so far into the back of his head that she was worried that they might get stuck there.

49. She gave the sales assistant a tight-lipped smile, but it was a defense mechanism; her eyes were laced with fury.

50. He squinted so hard that it seemed like he couldn't see anything at all.

51. She scrunched her mouth into a tight circle on the side of her face.

52. He made a big show of scraping the goo from the corner of his eye, even though it was three in the afternoon.

53. She gave him a long, slow blink, then sighed.

Actions

54. He was about to say something stupid, so he pretended to take a big gulp from his empty cup.

55. She tapped her heels impatiently on the tile floor, but no-one seemed to notice.

56. He decided that the middle of their conversation was the perfect time to pull out his phone and check his messages.

57. She laughed out loud, then realized that he hadn't been joking; he really thought that his problems were more serious than hers.

58. He leaned on his horn, even though the light had just changed and there were four cars between him and the intersection.

59. When he told her that he had been fired, she just shrugged, as if to say, "welcome to my world."

60. He gathered a mouthful of saliva and spat on the ground between them, knowing full well that she detested the habit.

Jealousy

Jealousy is part of anger because someone can become angry when another person possesses something that is desired. Not possessing it consumes the person and it makes them jealous of the other person such that they treat them as their enemy, even though there may not be any justifiable reason to do so.

A well-known story involving jealousy is 'Snow White and The Seven Dwarfs' by the Brothers Grimm. Snow White's step-mother is the Queen and she is jealous of Snow White's beauty, so she tries to kill her.

Jealousy can morph relationships that are supposed to be loving into ones of one-sided hatred.

Here's how you can *show* jealousy in your writing.

Surroundings

61. When they walked into the ballroom, everyone's heads turned; they just knew that everyone wanted to take the trophy away from them.

62. She trailed behind them by half a block, furious that her own family only paid attention to Sienna's troubles and ignored hers.

63. He hated that every other car in the parking lot was newer and nicer than his.

64. She was convinced that all of her coworkers went out and bought better shoes to make her nicest pair seem shabby.

65. He wanted to make the other kids cry, so that they would know how he felt every day.

66. She was even envious of the pairs of birds in the trees. If they could find somebody, why couldn't she?

67. He sat in the back row, praying for rain. That would put an end to their cosy beach gathering.

Appearance

68. His eyes turned green and without flinching, he stared at it like a man possessed.

69. She knew that now was an appropriate time to smile, but she just couldn't do it.

70. While he managed to force his mouth into a U-shape smile, underneath, he gritted his teeth and clenched his jaw tightly.

71. She tried to congratulate them warmly, but her eyes were like dead pools of ash.

72. John glared at his triumphant rival, but it didn't matter: he had won.

73. She hoped that her face wasn't betraying how badly she felt like throwing up that very second.

Actions

74. He couldn't muster any words of congratulation but instead scowled and muttered something to himself as he walked away shaking his head.

75. She told her former best friend that she was lucky to find such cute shoes in such a grotesquely large size.

76. He almost crumpled up the invitation and threw it at his father's head, but he stopped himself just in time.

77. She never learned how to accept defeat with grace. Instead, she folded her arms and pouted like a toddler.

78. When they announced that the other actor had won the award, he stood up and left the theater, heading straight for the nearest exit.

79. Her hands became knives as she reduced the letter into shreds—it wasn't possible that they offered her spot to someone else.

80. Every time Rachel walked past, Emily made it a point to stand outside and loudly mock her appearance but inside, Emily wanted everything that Rachel owned.

Provocation

A character becomes provoked when another character deliberately makes them annoyed or angry. It is different from other forms of anger because it is a reaction to other peoples' behavior, rather than something that comes about organically. This makes it a particularly useful emotion to bring almost any scene to the next level of intensity.

Good dialogue depends on conflict, and provocation is a common result of that conflict. It can manifest itself in many different ways, from physical and verbal outbursts to more subtle changes in a character's demeanor, but if you can get the idea of provocation across, you can bet that your readers will keep turning pages!

Below, you'll find some examples of the different ways that you can use provocation in your own work.

Surroundings

81. Even the magazines on the coffee table seemed to be deliberately placed there to annoy her.

82. He was certain that the universe was conspiring against him; it started to rain the moment he said that he didn't need an umbrella.

83. She wanted to get away as quickly as possible, but the ice caked onto her windshield made that impossible.

84. He couldn't help but think that the sun was shining just to spite him.

85. She looked at the happy faces on the billboard, grinning at her misfortune.

86. He fished a few cents out of his pocket and they were filthy—further proof that his germaphobia was ridiculous.

87. She took the stairs two at a time to show that she was still in good shape, but she stopped halfway up, panting, unable to catch her breath.

Appearance

88. He gritted his teeth, trying not to show his irritation.

89. She let her jaw go slack, then snapped it shut.

90. He winced involuntarily, then tried to cover it up with a yawn.

91. She tried to keep from reacting, but her raised eyebrows gave her away.

92. His smile looked more like an animal baring its teeth.

93. She wanted to scream, but contented herself with a quiet click of her tongue.

Actions

94. He stared at his adversary and cracked his knuckles.

95. Bristling at her touch, she shrugged Rachel's hand off her shoulders— she was no longer a friend.

96. He smiled as sincerely as possible, but he couldn't keep his brow from twitching.

97. She rolled her eyes, trying her best to act like she wasn't disappointed, but the sadness in her eyes gave her away.

98. He raised his hand and volunteered, desperate to prove that he wasn't scared of public speaking.

99. She deliberately slowed down, unwilling to let a tailgater decide her speed.

100. He coughed into his arm nonchalantly, hoping to blame the tears brimming in his eyes on allergies.

Resentment

Resentment is another form of anger that you can utilize in your stories. A character becomes resentful when they are feeling hurt or indignant, usually because they believe that they have been treated unfairly.

It is somewhat similar to provocation, in that it is a reaction to other characters' behavior, but it manifests itself more subtly, as sadness or bitterness, instead of as aggression.

Resentment can be very powerful in almost any scene, because it can serve as an early indication of your character's later actions. For example, say one character mocks another for driving a broken-down car. If the driver is shown to be resentful of these comments, it will make sense to the reader when he lets the air out of his rival's tires later on.

Since resentment can be very effective for foreshadowing purposes, it is an essential weapon in any writer's arsenal. Here are some more ways that you can use resentment in your stories:

Surroundings

101. Suddenly he felt a chill, although it was a beautiful sunny day.

102. As if on cue, a raincloud burst above her, even though she could see that it was still dry two blocks away.

103. He looked around the room. It seemed like every single person was wearing nicer clothes than him.

104. She just knew that he put her cereal on the top shelf—where she couldn't reach it, even on tiptoe—deliberately.

105. The bank offered him a measly two hundred dollar loan; he stormed out the door rather than signing the paperwork.

106. It was as if every item in his expensively-furnished apartment was hand-picked to make her jealous.

107. He saw the lawyer smirk as he signed the contract, already knowing that he was making the wrong decision.

Appearance

108. She accepted his backhanded compliment with a tight-lipped smile.

109. He wiped the tears from the corners of his eyes, blaming them on the wind.

110. She responded to the announcement with a dead-eyed stare.

111. His face twisted into an expression of agony, as if her words were causing him physical pain.

112. She grinned and then laughed, even though nobody had said anything remotely funny.

113. He pretended like his frown was just a result of his concentrating on the meaning of the fine print.

Actions

114. She thanked him for his time, then turned and almost jogged out of the room.

115. He gave the parking ticket a cursory glance, then stuffed it into his pocket like a used tissue.

116. She pretended to trip over his brand new white shoes, but she hoped that her dirty black heels left a scuff mark.

117. He crossed the street before the light changed, just because he knew it would irritate his mother.

118. She didn't even bother to thank her customers for the handful of change that they gave her as a tip.

119. She told him that she hoped he would find their agreement acceptable; he just shrugged and pulled out his phone.

120. She made sure to step in every puddle she passed on the way to his apartment, hoping to track dirt all across his white carpeting.

Sarcasm

Sarcasm is a mild form of anger that uses irony in an attempt to mock someone or to show contempt for them. A person's response is considered sarcastic if it deliberately expresses the opposite of their opinion, especially in a negative way. While it can sometimes be difficult to convey sarcasm without the proper context, if you can successfully master this emotion, it can achieve very entertaining and nuanced results in your stories.

Like resentment, sarcasm can only occur as a character's reaction to the situation at hand.

However, its goals are different; while resentment is usually somewhat hidden from its intended target, sarcasm is meant to be recognized by the offending party.

This can allow the stakes of a conversation to be ramped up on both sides, which can lead to a lot of thinly veiled hostility, and make the reader excited to see what's going to happen next.

Let's take a look at some examples of different types of sarcasm that you can use in your own writing.

Surroundings

121. Of course he left his house without an umbrella on the only rainy afternoon of the month; today was going to be just perfect.

122. She stepped in dog poop while crossing the street and practically cheered; at least nothing could get any worse.

123. When the cashier told him that his third credit card had also been declined, he started to laugh in spite of himself.

124. After paying the tow truck driver to get her car back, she thanked him profusely for saving her from holding the parking spot five minutes longer than she was supposed to.

125. When the power went out, he pulled out a book and strained his eyes to read in the darkness, unwilling to let the universe dictate his evening routine.

126. The sign said "do not walk on the grass," so she started jogging.

127. The battery in his watch died months ago, but whenever anyone asked him the time he would dutifully look at it and tell them that it was a quarter past twelve.

Appearance

128. She rolled her eyes theatrically.

129. He raised an eyebrow and gave her a sideways glance.

130. She furrowed her brow and pouted at the good news.

131. He smiled like he had just seen a video of three kittens playing with each other.

132. She knew that she should be sympathetic, but she just tilted her head back and laughed so hard that she had to catch her breath.

133. He pursed his lips and blinked.

Actions

134. He missed the elevator, and gave the guy holding the "door close" button a big thumbs up.

135. She made sure to give the hairdresser who shaved off her eyebrow a generous tip.

136. He started clapping when he saw his friend trip over the curb.

137. She wrote a polite note thanking the man for blocking her car in, and left it under his windshield wiper.

138. He threw the fifteen dollars that he had earned that week into the air and did a little dance as they rained down around him.

139. She asked the dry cleaner if he could add bleach stains to the rest of her white blouses, too.

140. He feigned exaggerated concern for the rich man who had misplaced his third favorite pair of cufflinks.

Violation

Violation is a type of anger that occurs when a character feels that someone has disrespected his or her privacy, rights, or peace.

When a character feels violated, he or she may mistrust others, fear for his or her safety, or react in strange ways to situations that remind him or her of the original violation. This emotion can be very helpful for writers, because it results in a change in the character.

There are many different situations that can result in a character feeling violated, but we will focus on a basic version of the feeling to help show how you can use it in your own work. Here is the example: Lydia has learned that Hank, her father, has read her diary without permission. This act makes her feel violated because she thought that her diary was a place where she could express her thoughts and feelings in private. After she learns about this violation of her trust, Lydia has trouble believing that anything in her life can be private.

Surroundings

141. Each morning, Lydia found something out of place in her room, something that could have been moved overnight.

142. Lydia was afraid to make phone calls at home, convinced that Hank could be listening in on the other line.

143. Lydia began taking strange, erratic routes to school, hoping to shake anyone tailing her.

144. It seemed like dark shadows followed Lydia everywhere she went, witnessing her secrets, laughing at her helplessness.

145. Every night, Lydia tried to fall asleep on the couch, because she didn't feel safe in her own room anymore.

146. Lydia felt like a prisoner in her own town, always being watched, never being left alone.

147. There was a security camera in front of the bank across the street; whenever she passed by it, Lydia buried her face in her jacket, trying to hide her identity.

Appearance

148. Lydia scowled at Hank and refused to eat his peace offering of ice cream.

149. Lydia narrowed her eyes and frowned, certain that this was another trap.

150. Whenever Hank tried to explain why he read her diary, Lydia's eye started to twitch, and her lips began trembling.

151. Lydia's eyes darted back and forth, scanning the living room for potential spies.

152. Lydia furrowed her brow and squinted, making sure that nobody was hiding in the hallway.

153. Lydia stared at her father with wide eyes, wondering why he would do this to her.

Actions

154. Lydia bit her lip and lifted up her pillow, worried that her diary wasn't where she had left it.

155. Lydia ripped up the note into tiny pieces and flushed it down the toilet.

156. Lydia's teacher caught her trying to pass a note in class; she told Lydia to give the note to her, but she balled it up and stuck it in her mouth, afraid that the teacher might tell her dad about the subject of the message.

157. On her way to school, Lydia kept checking over her shoulder to make sure that she wasn't being followed.

158. Lydia cut the middle section out of an old dictionary on her bookshelf, and hid her diary inside the empty space.

159. Lydia tried to calm herself down, but she couldn't stop hyperventilating.

160. Lydia knew that she was acting crazy, but that didn't prevent her from checking her bedroom for cameras and microphones.

CHAPTER THREE

Anticipation

Anticipation is the act of looking forward. You can look forward to something positive in your life or even foresee a negative event.

There are different levels of anticipation—you could be hopeful of a much wanted outcome and you can also be waiting eagerly.

Anticipation helps you, as the writer, to build up to a major event. It helps you hook in the reader so that they read on in order to find out what happens next.

In this chapter, you're going to see how you can express, in words, different levels and types of anticipation for the characters in your story.

Confidence

A form of anticipation for every writer to master is confidence—a positive forward outlook that believes that good possibilities will eventuate.

A character is confident when they have a high sense of their own self-worth, ability, or proficiency. Confident characters can take advantage of their situations, and change things in their favor. They often become leaders or mentors, helping other, less confident characters realize that they have potential.

It is important to include confident characters in almost any story, because they help you show your readers that you are in control of the situation. If everybody is skeptical and doubtful of their own abilities, nothing will ever get done, and your characters will never change.

Often, the best way to increase the confidence of a character is by letting a more confident character mentor him, so that they can turn their potential into greatness. The student-master dynamic has been a common theme throughout literature, and it is directly rooted in confidence!

Here is a simple example of confidence that you can use as a template for your own work: Melissa is a novice painter. She is very talented, but doesn't think that her work is any good. Then she meets Karen, a famous painter who sees potential in Melissa's work and takes her under her wing. Through their interactions, Melissa's confidence in the value of her work increases.

Surroundings

161. When she set up her easel next to Karen's, paint just seemed to flow from her fingertips right onto the canvas.

162. Melissa watched Karen observe her newest painting, thrilled that she didn't pick it up and throw it into the trash.

163. Karen never seemed to make a mistake, or to come up with a bad idea; everything about her exuded perfection.

164. On the way home from Karen's studio, Melissa would often feel like she was being carried on a breeze. Everything was worth painting, everything was beautiful.

165. Melissa soon learned to judge her work based on that of her peers, not the greatest painters that ever lived.

166. Instead of constantly putting herself down, Melissa began to have dreams that she was the most famous painter on Earth; her work was hanging in galleries all over the world.

167. One of Melissa's paintings was selected for a local gallery opening. Seeing it on the wall next to other peoples' art validated the whole pursuit for her; she was going to have more paintings in galleries, no matter what it took.

Appearance

168. Karen's smile was self-contented and natural; she probably didn't even realize that she was doing it.

169. Even though the critic was tearing her work apart, Karen looked perfectly serene and calm.

170. Melissa kept her chin up and raised an eyebrow, unwilling to let the man know that he'd insulted her.

171. Melissa's eyes became sharp and unyielding; she was determined not to let any of these lessons slip past her.

172. Instead of saying something self-deprecating, Melissa responded to the compliment with a little half-smile and a nod.

173. Melissa looked disheveled and exhausted—you could tell that she hadn't slept properly in days—but her eyes were more alive and awake than ever.

Actions

174. Melissa used to be too embarrassed to paint in public; now she set up her tools on the sidewalk, happy to be working outdoors for a change.

175. Melissa walked with her head high and her shoulders back; she looked like she had grown six inches overnight.

176. Instead of spying on the artist she saw sketching in his notebook at the cafe, like she normally would, Melissa walked straight up to him and asked about his shading technique.

177. Melissa painted enthusiastically and deliberately, not concentrating on what the final image would be, but trusting her instincts to lead her down the right path.

178. Melissa strode right up to the internationally famous photographer and shook his hand warmly.

179. Melissa made sure that the gallery patrons all knew that the painting hanging on the wall behind her was hers.

180. Melissa began to make conversation with people in museums and art supply stores, picking their brains about art history and painting techniques.

Courage

One type of anticipation that a character can experience is courage.

It's a form of anticipation that is brave. A character may anticipate that a particular action will lead to a loss, but they may look forward in a way that is courageous and brave.

A character feels courageous when they act in a way that ignores the potential of danger or suffering, in the name of a cause. This behavior is often rewarded by the character's peers, which in turn makes them feel happy for standing up for what they believe in.

Courage is a very powerful tool for fiction writers. The best stories all have serious conflicts and high stakes; they put characters into situations that most ordinary people would not be able to overcome. Thus, a courageous character, one who is able to ignore their own personal safety and act in superhuman ways to help others, is a great way to resolve a difficult plot line.

Acts of courage are action-packed and suspenseful, and all readers love them; if you can harness this feeling in your own work, you'll be sure to keep your audience turning pages!

Here is a scenario that involves courageous behavior: Walter is a regular, timid guy. One day, he walks down the street and realizes that an apartment building is on fire, and there is a baby trapped inside of a room. Instead of waiting for help to arrive, Walter acts, charging into the building and saving the day.

Surroundings

181. Suddenly, Walter couldn't feel the heat, or see the world around him; all that mattered was that baby.

182. Walter felt his heart skip a beat; he wanted to get away from the building, but his feet wouldn't budge.

183. Visions of every time that Walter missed an opportunity to do something great floated in front of him, one after the other.

184. Walter could hear sirens wailing far in the distance, but he knew that they weren't nearly close enough to save the people trapped inside.

185. Time seemed to crawl to a halt; Walter had centuries to decide what to do, to iron out all of the kinks in his plan.

186. The sky was filled with smoke, but a thin beacon of sun broke through, hitting Walter like a spotlight.

187. When he emerged from the building, covered in soot and carrying the baby, the crowd erupted into cheers.

Appearance

188. Walter's face was utterly neutral, expressionless; he'd made up his mind.

189. Walter gritted his teeth and squinted through the smoke.

190. Walter shielded his eyes from the light of the flames, using his hand as a visor.

191. Walter frowned and furrowed his brow in concentration, knowing that he was already past the point of no return.

192. Walter's eyes were bloodshot and wild, but he still grinned when he finally found the baby.

193. Even though he was freaking out inside, Walter's face was the picture of calm. He caught his reflection in a sooty mirror in the hallway; he was even smiling a little.

Actions

194. Walter barreled into the building, busting open locked doors with his shoulder.

195. Walter covered his face with his shirt, but the thick smoke was still choking him.

196. Walter grabbed the door handle, then his hand jerked back automatically; it was red hot.

197. Walter wanted to crouch down on the floor and rest for a moment, but he kept moving; he knew that that would have been the last mistake he ever made.

198. Walter wasn't sure that he would survive the fall, but he jumped out the third story window anyway, clutching the baby to his chest; it was his only hope of survival.

199. Walter felt the hair burning off of his arms, but still he pressed forward, unafraid.

200. Walter knew that he only had a few minutes before the smoke would overpower him, so he stuck his head out the window, took a deep breath, and ran upstairs as fast as he could.

Eagerness

One of the most positive forms of anticipation is eagerness. A character feels eager when they want to do something so badly that they start becoming impatient and anxious, or experiencing intense hope and yearning.

Eager characters will often lose control of their ability to behave normally, and begin to act frantic and childish in spite of themselves. This can often result in humorous situations, especially if the eager character is normally very serious and stern.

Eagerness is a great emotion for storytellers to capitalize on. It helps illustrate that the character is really excited about—and invested in—his or her current situation, which makes scenes more impactful and entertaining. By showing that the events taking place really matter to your character, you make them feel more human and realistic, which is always a good thing!

Here is a simple example of eagerness that you can use as a guide for your own work: Jack has always wanted a dog, and after months of begging and doing his chores, his parents have finally agreed to take him to the pet store.

Surroundings

201. Seeing the pet shop come into focus through the car window felt like catching a glimpse of Heaven itself.

202. Ever since his parents announced the pet store trip, it felt like the clock was moving at half speed. An hour seemed like an eternity.

203. Jack spent the afternoon daydreaming about all the fun that he would have with a new puppy.

204. Jack was so excited that he couldn't focus on anything else; he just sat in the corner with his shoes and jacket on, ready to jump into the car at a moment's notice.

205. Jack spent the endlessly long afternoon brainstorming names for the puppy with a huge smile on his face.

206. Jack knew that he should try to calm himself down, but it took every ounce of his self control to keep from bouncing off the walls and screaming.

207. Jack was so happy that he was verging on panic; he nearly started to hyperventilate.

Appearance

208. Jack smiled so wide that his jaw started to click whenever he opened it.

209. When Jack's parents told him he could have a dog, his eyebrows shot up and his jaw dropped.

210. Jack bit the inside of his cheek to keep from squealing out of sheer joy.

211. Jack's eyes darted wildly from one puppy to the other; they were both so perfect, how was he ever going to choose?

212. Jack was alert, sharp-eyed and smiling; this was the greatest moment of his entire life.

213. Jack kept staring off into space with his tongue sticking out of the corner of his mouth, imagining the moment that he would bring home his very own dog.

Actions

214. Jack killed some time by making a long list of all the pet supplies and toys that he'd have to pick up at the store, checking it several times to make sure that he hadn't forgotten anything.

215. Jack spent an hour babbling about dogs in the kitchen before his mom told him to go play outside.

216. Jack kept wringing his hands and glancing up at the clock, counting down the minutes until he would get to pick out a puppy.

217. Jack frantically rearranged his room over and over again, trying to find the perfect place for a dog bed.

218. Jack's mind was racing with impatience; he sat crosslegged on the floor and tried to breathe evenly, hoping to slow himself down a little, but it was no use.

219. Jack was able to calm down temporarily by surfing through about a thousand dog pictures online, but after a while it just made him even more excited.

220. Jack went outside and sat on the hood of the car a full half hour before his parents had said they'd be leaving for the pet store.

Energy

Another way that characters can respond to anticipation is by feeling energetic. Energetic characters show a lot of vitality and liveliness; they are often difficult to calm down or control. Like eagerness, increased energy usually comes from positive anticipation, but it shows itself in a much more physical way.

Energetic characters can be effective in all sorts of stories. They tend to become impulsive and impatient, which means that they could put themselves into situations without fully thinking about possible consequences. This tendency towards risk-taking can take your scenes in fun and unexpected directions, which will result in faster pacing and increased reader attention.

Here is an example of an energetic character that you can use as a basis for your own stories: Elise was having a quiet night at home when Kate, her best friend from preschool, burst through the door unannounced. Elise hadn't seen Kate in years, and Kate felt incredibly excited and energetic to surprise her friend.

Surroundings

221. Kate checked the time—it was a quarter to one in the morning. Normally, she would have been in bed long ago, but sleep was the last thing on her mind.

222. Elise wasn't exactly prepared for a night on the town, but it wasn't every day that Kate showed up on her doorstep. After she'd gotten over the initial shock of seeing her friend, she started frantically searching the internet, checking to see if any of their favorite bands were playing nearby.

223. Kate had always had a strange effect on Elise; she couldn't remember the last time that she'd felt so perky and motivated.

224. There were so many things that Elise had to tell Kate about that she didn't know where to start, she just kept rambling on, bouncing from tangent to tangent.

225. Elise was already sure that they were going to stay up until sunrise.

226. Elise was so worked up that she could practically hear her brain whirring in her ears.

227. Even after a very long night of running around and acting crazy, Elise was so excited that she had trouble falling asleep.

Appearance

228. Elise's eyes were wide open, and her pupils were like pinpricks; she looked like she had just chugged down two large bottles of soda.

229. Elise grinned from ear to ear and nodded rapidly as Kate caught her up on her recent past.

230. Elise couldn't remember the last time she'd blinked, but it must have been a while ago because her eyes felt bloodshot and dry.

231. Elise raised her eyebrows and laughed wildly whenever Kate told her a funny story.

232. Elise bit her lip and scanned the room, searching for a new topic of conversation.

233. Elise beamed when Kate suggested that she brew some coffee; the night was only beginning.

Actions

234. Elise couldn't sit still; her leg was fidgeting uncontrollably.

235. Elise was so thrilled to talk to Kate again that her teeth started chattering in between sentences.

236. Elise was full of excitement that she paced around her apartment for an hour, talking to Kate nonstop, hoping to calm herself down a little bit.

237. Elise felt like she could do a cartwheel right now. In fact, she did do one, right in the middle of her hallway.

238. Elise started chewing on her fingernail absent-mindedly; she needed to get out of this apartment and find an outlet for this liveliness before she drove herself crazy.

239. Elise kept drumming her fingers on the countertop; all of this excitement was beginning to make her feel antsy.

240. Elise tackled Kate in a bear hug and screamed, "Oh my goodness! I can't believe you're here!"

Hope

Another important variation of anticipation is hope.

A character is hopeful when they feel optimistic about the future. After a situation ends well for a character, they may become hopeful, and believe that things are going to continue to work out for them. This belief can be confirmed or denied later on in the story; either way, it will evoke a powerful reaction from the character.

Hope can be a very effective tool for writers to use. If a story is destined to end tragically, giving your main character a hopeful outlook in the middle of the piece will make their ultimate failure much more impactful. If you're headed for a happy ending, gradually allowing your protagonist to become more and more hopeful will reinforce their ultimate triumph.

Both of these techniques will increase your readers' investment in your story, which is essential to its success.

Here is a basic example of hopefulness that you can use as a model: Clare is running for a student council position at her school. At first, she thought that she would definitely lose to a more popular student, but as her campaign moves forward, more and more of her classmates have told her that she has their vote.

Surroundings

241. At lunch, three different students that Clare had never met pledged to vote for her. The rest of the day floated by in a happy blur; she might just have a chance, after all.

242. Clare could hear people at the other table talking about what a great candidate she was, even though they had no idea that she was sitting there.

243. Clare used to wish on shooting stars, but tonight, she let one fly past without asking for anything; she had all the luck she needed.

244. The day of the election, Clare was greeted with cheers when she walked into the auditorium.

245. Even when she was away from school, it felt like people in town were treating Clare with much more respect than they once did.

246. Little things that used to irritate Clare no longer bothered her; she was doing something important, and that put everything into perspective.

247. Clare stood in the corner and observed the students lined up at the voting booth; it was going to be close, but it seemed like at least half of them were wearing buttons with her face on them.

Appearance

248. Clare blushed and raked her hair out of her eyes; she wasn't used to being publicly complimented.

249. Clare grinned and raised an eyebrow, glad to see that her campaign was gaining supporters.

250. Clare looked around the room with widened eyes; she couldn't believe that people were going through all of this trouble just for her.

251. Clare's bright eyes and easy smile showed that she was ready to overcome every obstacle in her path.

252. Clare's mouth opened and she gasped as she looked around the hallway; her friends had taped up her posters everywhere.

253. Clare closed her eyes and let the contentment wash over her, as a slow smile crept across her face.

Actions

254. When Clare was certain that she was the last one left in the classroom, she jumped around in a circle and squealed; it was really happening.

255. Clare walked up to her opponent and shook his hand warmly; she knew that she had a good chance of winning, and that boosted her confidence.

256. Clare started arriving at school early, so that she could speak with the other students as they trickled in the front door to convince them that she was the best one for the job.

257.Clare wasn't sure that anyone would take her fliers, but after an hour, she had passed them all out. People even stopped and chatted with her, wishing her good luck in the election.

258. Clare started to dress up a little for school; she was acting like a politician, so she might as well look like one.

259. At the debate, Clare decided to leave her notecards in her pocket; she was already prepared, she didn't need a cheat sheet to help her make her points.

260. Clare began to tutor struggling students after class, hoping that others would follow her lead and help to make their school a better place.

Inspiration

One version of anticipation that is crucial in many stories is inspiration. A character feels inspired when they feel motivated to do or feel something, especially something creative.

Inspiration will make characters anticipate positive futures in ways that they normally wouldn't, but the focus of inspiration is usually the creation of something. Inspired characters will often make up stories or songs, or begin to paint, as an outlet for the other emotions that have overtaken them.

An often-repeated piece of advice for new writers is "write what you know." For this reason, inspiration is a common emotion throughout literature.

Many famous characters are writers, musicians, painters, and other artists, because writers can identify with these people at a deep level and bring their ideas and feelings to life.

Topics like writer's block, the therapeutic power of creativity, and the euphoria of making something can be found in most stories in one way or another, and they all involve inspiration. If you can portray this feeling successfully, you can make your readers feel inspired themselves, which is a noble and rewarding goal.

Here is an example of a situation that revolves around inspiration: Kathleen is a writer. For months, she has suffered from a terrible case of writer's block; nothing has seemed like a good idea for a story. Just when she was about to give up hope and stop writing altogether, Kathleen is hit by a burst of inspiration, and suddenly she can write for hours on end without struggling.

Surroundings

261. Kathleen smiled when she heard the birds chirping outside her window; she couldn't remember the last time that she'd stayed up all night writing.

262. Suddenly, every conversation that Kathleen had, every interaction she witnessed on the street, directly related to her idea. No little detail seemed pointless, everything was falling right into place.

263. Kathleen could picture scenes playing out in front of her; the ideas were flowing faster than she could write them down.

264. In the space of six hours, Kathleen had written twice as much as she had all year; she was exhausted, but she felt like she could fly.

265. People kept asking Kathleen if she'd changed her hair, or bought new clothes; everything about her was positively glowing.

266. Kathleen knew that this burst of creativity wouldn't last forever, so she tried to take advantage of every second of it.

267. Kathleen had stopped straightening her apartment and doing her laundry; the whole place was a wreck, but she didn't care. None of that was important now.

Appearance

268. Kathleen's mouth was hanging open and her skin was blotchy and pale, but her eyes were more alive than they'd ever been.

269. An hour into her frantic typing session, Kathleen's jaw started to hurt; she realized that she'd been grinning the entire time.

270. Kathleen's eyes darted around the page and she kept nodding to herself over and over again; she was definitely on the right track.

271. Kathleen's hair was greasy from skipping a few days of showers, but her bright eyes and easy smile made her look more beautiful than ever.

272. Tears streamed down Kathleen's face, but she was smiling; she'd finally had an idea.

273. Kathleen stuck her tongue out of the side of her mouth and squinted at the screen, lost in concentration.

Actions

274. Kathleen started carrying a notebook around in her purse; so many ideas came to her during the day that she was afraid she'd forget them before she got home.

275. Kathleen's fingers ached and her eyes stung from staring into her computer screen all day, but she was so excited to be writing again that she barely even noticed.

276. At work, Kathleen would hide in the bathroom for hours at a time, scribbling in her notebook.

277. It was 2pm before Kathleen realized that she'd forgotten to eat lunch. She heated up a cup of noodles and ate it at her desk, unwilling to take a break to make a proper meal.

278. Kathleen walked around the town square with her head on a swivel, eavesdropping on peoples' conversations and soaking in all the details that popped out at her.

279. Kathleen started to carry around a tape recorder, in order to capture her thoughts as they were occurring to her.

280. At the end of the week, Kathleen had written over a hundred pages. She printed it all out and began to correct it with a red pen; it wasn't all brilliant, but there was definitely something there.

CHAPTER FOUR

Disgust

Everybody feels disgusted sometimes. This feeling can happen for lots of reasons: maybe you see something that grosses you out, like worms or spiders; maybe someone does something to you that makes you not want to spend time with them anymore; maybe you hear about something that someone did in the past that makes you think that they aren't a good person.

Whatever the reason for it, disgust can be a very important feeling to capture in your stories. If a character is disgusted, he or she will react very strongly to whatever is making him or her feel that way. This can make any scene more interesting, and help to show your character's opinion of the people around them.

This chapter will discuss many different types of disgust, some of them intense and other ones comparatively mild. By the end, you should have a pretty good idea of some ways to use this feeling in your own work.

Aversion

The first type of disgust that we will illustrate for you is aversion. Aversion is a feeling of strong dislike or disinterest. When a character feels aversion for a person or situation, he or she will do anything to avoid it. This can be useful in fiction because it can lead to unexpected twists in your stories.

There are countless situations that can lead to aversion, but we will focus on a simple one to illustrate the emotion. Following an extended illness that nearly killed her, Rebecca develops an aversion to all germs and dirtiness. This condition makes it very difficult for her to interact with people physically, or to spend time in places that aren't spotlessly clean.

Surroundings

281. In her imagination, every surface was caked with soot and grime.

282. Rebecca pictured germs writhing like worms on the doorknob.

283. Everywhere she went, it seemed like people were deliberately coughing and sneezing in her direction.

284. Filth and disease were closing in on her from every direction; she had to get out of there.

285. Rebecca used to think that her mother was a neat freak; now, her house looked like a pig sty.

286. She knew that the doctor's office was one of the most sanitary places that she could ever go, but ever since her illness, its smell of disinfectant and latex gloves reminded her of death.

287. A light snow had started to fall. Once, she would have loved to take a peaceful walk among the flurries; now, the thought of the dirty frozen water touching her made her skin crawl.

Appearance

288. Rebecca screwed her eyes shut and pursed her lips tight to avoid gagging.

289. Rebecca's skin turned a shade of green, and her eyes started to water a little.

290. She stared at the dirty napkin on the table intensely, as if it might jump at her the second she stopped paying attention to it.

291. She scrunched up her nose and tried to breathe through her mouth, in order to keep from smelling the garbage down the alley.

292. Rebecca's jaw dropped at the sight of the mouse scurrying across the kitchen floor.

293. Rebecca squinted until her eyes were pinpricks and tucked her chin to her neck, desperate to stop the rain from touching her face.

Actions

294. Although she detested littering, Rebecca let the receipt that had fallen out of her pocket blow down the street, rather than picking it up once it touched the ground.

295. Rebecca's nose itched like crazy, but she refused to scratch it because she knew that she hadn't washed her hands for an hour.

296. Rebecca turned up the heat in the shower until her skin was red and raw.

297. Rebecca started to wear gloves whenever she left her house, even in the middle of summer.

298. When the child started staggering towards her with his grubby hands outstretched, Rebecca turned and literally ran in the opposite direction.

299. A car drove past and splashed through a dirty puddle, covering her from head to toe. Rebecca stood on the corner for fifteen minutes, twitching and crying in the rain.

300. When she finally made it home, Rebecca washed her hands in the sink for twenty minutes straight.

Boredom

One comparatively mild form of disgust is boredom. A character feels bored when they are disinterested in everything that is happening around them, full of apathy and ennui.

This emotion displays itself as a general malaise that temporarily overcomes the character, and is often accompanied by a lot of complaining. Bored characters are desperate to find anything to relieve their boredom, so they aren't usually bored for very long.

Boredom can be a very useful emotion for writers to illustrate, particularly in the beginnings of stories. Every story needs to start somewhere, and a character who is bored will often seek out adventure and excitement to spice things up.

The obstacles and implications of any journey will help to give their life meaning, and they will soon forget that they were ever bored. Everyone has experienced this emotion, which makes it easy for your audience to sympathize with bored characters, and feel happy for them once their life starts to become more exciting.

Let's take a look at a simple example of boredom that you can use to help you portray the emotion in your own writing: Kyle's family has gone to a resort town on vacation, but he hates the beach. He spends the first few days lounging around the hotel feeling incredibly bored and very sorry for himself.

Surroundings

301. Kyle lay in bed staring at the ceiling for what felt like hours, but when he glanced over at the alarm clock, only fifteen minutes had passed; the dullness made his skin crawl.

302. Kyle would rather study for a math class or watch paint dry than spend another day sitting at the beach, but there were still four days to go.

303. Kyle wished that he could sleep for a week straight and wake up on the car ride back home.

304. Every time Kyle looked out the window, it was the same view again—sand and sea—the entire vacation was designed for him to have as little fun as possible.

305. The heat of the summer sun made time pass even slower, like everything was moving in slow motion.

306. Kyle started daydreaming about parties and video games and air conditioning, but it didn't make him feel any less trapped and weary.

307. There was a huge bookshelf in the hotel lobby; Kyle decided to organize the entire thing in alphabetical order, but by the time he was finished there were still four hours before sundown.

Appearance

308. Kyle rolled his eyes and groaned; he felt like he was trapped in a waiting room.

309. Kyle looked like a zombie; his eyes were glazed over and his shoulders were stooped, like his boredom was a burden that he had to carry around on his back.

310. Kyle closed his eyes and sighed, trying to keep from getting exasperated.

311. When Kyle's father asked him if he was having fun, he put on his most patronizing grin and nodded rapidly.

312. Kyle frowned and knocked his head against the wall. The monotony was starting to drive him crazy.

313. Kyle rubbed his temples and winced, wishing that he could just go home and take a nap.

Actions

314. Kyle's family left to beat the crowds to the beach, but he stayed at the hotel, playing solitaire and wishing that he were anywhere else in the world.

315. Kyle had brought three books with him, but he'd read through them all by the end of the third day.

316. Kyle started to count ceiling tiles in the hotel room, but he kept messing up and losing count halfway through.

317. Kyle decided to go for a swim; he hadn't given the ocean a fair chance. He was back on the blanket three minutes later, shivering and smelling like seaweed.

318. Kyle started wandering around town aimlessly, hoping to find somewhere worth going. He gave up when nothing fun presented itself before dinnertime.

319. Kyle spent most of the day texting his friends. They told him about all the hijinks that they were getting into back home to try to cheer him up, but it only made him feel worse.

320. Kyle decided to pass the time by balancing on one foot for as long as possible, but he got sick of the game after an hour or so.

Conceit

One interesting type of disgust that a character can display is conceit. A character is conceited when they have excessive pride and vanity in themselves.

This type of self-obsession almost always occurs in relation to others; rather than simply thinking highly of themselves, a conceited character regards others as inferior to them. This means that they are constantly looking down on the people around them, expressing disgust and disapproval of their habits and lifestyles.

Conceited characters can be very useful as villains, because they can be irrationally mean to everybody else in the story, which makes it easy for readers to root against them.

There are countless ways to show conceit in fiction, but let's look at a simple example to illustrate this feeling effectively. Bill comes from a wealthy family, but he is staying with his comparatively poor cousins over the summer. Since he is conceited, he feels the need to constantly compare his relatives' modest home and belongings to his own.

Surroundings

321. The house was tiny and pathetic; Bill's bedroom at home was double its size.

322. His cousins' living room was a joke; he didn't realize that they still made TVs with antennas on them.

323. Bill wondered what they did for fun in this backwoods town; after all, tipping cows must get old eventually.

324. When his cousin told him that they washed their dishes by hand, Bill thought that she was kidding, but he didn't see a dishwasher anywhere.

325. Bill strutted down the street, proud to be the only kid in sight wearing designer jeans.

326. At dinner, Bill held his fork up to the light; it wasn't even made of real silver!

327. If his friends back home saw him riding around in his cousins' rusty old station wagon, they would never let him live it down.

Appearance

328. Bill raised an eyebrow and sneered.

329. Bill turned up his nose and looked at the leftovers like they might start to move.

330. Bill rolled his eyes and laughed at his cousin's naïveté.

331. Bill took a deep breath and puffed out his cheeks as he stepped onto the public bus.

332. Bill winced and buried his face in his hands, unable to watch his cousin pay with change.

333. Bill clenched his jaw and squinted at the pullout couch he would have to sleep on for the next three months.

Actions

334. Bill picked up the secondhand sweater and held it at arm's length, afraid that he might catch lice.

335. Bill kept glancing over his shoulder, afraid that one of his cousins' poor neighbors might come up from behind and try to mug him.

336. Bill shook hands with his cousin's friend, then carefully wiped his palm on his jeans.

337. When Bill's cousin tripped over his shoes and scuffed them up, he demanded that she buy him a new pair.

338. The whole family spent the afternoon at the public pool, but Bill just sat in the corner and sulked the entire time.

339. Bill refused to play with his cousins' toys, because he already owned the same ones for years and he was tired of them.

340. Bill told his cousins that they should really hire a maid to clean up their house every once in a while.

Loathing

One of the strongest types of disgust is loathing. Loathing is a feeling of intense dislike or hatred. When one character loathes another, he or she cannot think of one redeeming quality that they have; they are irreconcilable enemies.

This can be a very useful emotion for writers to use, since a character that loathes another will never do anything to help them. They will behave in an openly hostile manner towards them, no matter what happens. This can add huge amounts of conflict to any situation, which always results in powerful and entertaining scenes.

Let's look at a specific example of loathing that you can use as a model for your own stories. Leslie has recently learned that her former best friend, Jill, has been playing with her sworn enemy and former friend, Anthony, behind her back. Leslie loathes both Jill and Anthony because of this betrayal. No matter what they do, Leslie will never trust them again.

Surroundings

341. Whenever Leslie was in the same room as Jill, she couldn't concentrate on anything else; she spent all of her energy sending waves of pure hatred in her direction.

342. The sky seemed to darken whenever she passed Anthony's house; she hoped that it would get struck by lightning.

343. Leslie would lie in bed fantasizing about the day that Anthony tricked Jill just as he did to her.

344. Leslie knew that Jill and Anthony felt bad about what happened, but she didn't care. She hoped that they would never get over it, that they would feel sad and guilty forever.

345. Leslie even started to hate some of her favorite songs, just because she and Anthony had once listened to them together.

346. It seemed like everywhere she looked, something reminded her of either Anthony or Jill, but that was okay, it only made her hatred stronger.

347. Leslie was sure that seeing Jill break down and cry would be the only thing that could make her feel better.

Appearance

348. Leslie glared at Anthony with hot coals for eyes.

349. Leslie curled her lip and sneered as Jill passed her in the parking lot.

350. Leslie bared her teeth at Anthony and almost snarled.

351. When she saw them laughing in the hallway, Leslie pursed her lips and narrowed her eyes into slits.

352. Leslie frowned and stared at him like he was a pile of rotting garbage.

353. Leslie could feel hot, angry tears forming at the corners of her eyes.

Actions

354. Jill tripped and skinned her knee in the hallway; Leslie just walked past her, laughing.

355. Leslie kicked a rock down the street, pretending that it was Anthony's head.

356. Leslie spent the afternoon tearing all of her old pictures of Jill into a million tiny pieces.

357. Leslie gathered up every gift that Anthony had ever given her and dumped them in a big pile in his front yard.

358. When she was assigned Jill as a partner for a group project, Leslie didn't even meet with her. They both received failing grades, but Leslie was happy because she brought Jill down with her.

359. At lunch, Jill brought Leslie her favorite dessert as a peace offering. Leslie smacked it out of her hands and it splattered all over Jill's new dress.

360. Leslie rammed her shoulder into Anthony as she brushed past him.

Revulsion

The last type of disgust that we'll illustrate is revulsion. A character feels revolted when they are sickened or nauseated by something. This strong, visceral dislike will often take the form of a physical reaction, like cringing or gagging.

When a character is revolted by something, they often can't stand to be close to it for long. This feeling can be helpful for writers to master, because it can be used as a unique trait to make any character feel more well-developed and realistic.

An otherwise normal or boring character that is revolted by something strange or interesting instantly becomes memorable, which makes them more entertaining for readers.

Characters can be revolted by all sorts of things, like foods, behaviors, or different types of animals.

Let's look at a specific example of this feeling: Wes is revolted by nose picking. No matter what else is happening, if he sees somebody picking his or her nose, he needs to leave the room or else he might be sick. This has been the case for as long as he can remember; he doesn't know why he feels so strongly about nose picking, but there's nothing that can make it gross him out any less.

Surroundings

361. Suddenly, it was like the room was spinning on an axis; he had to get out of here.

362. Wes tried to ignore the picking, but it was happening right in front of him; his vision narrowed to pinpricks and his face felt flushed.

363. It seemed that even the walls were covered with slimy and green snot and the thought of someone picking their nose made his stomach turn.

364. He felt acid lurching around in his throat; he needed to find a trash can, quick.

365. When his own nose itched, Wes did his best to ignore it, meditating on anything else that came to mind, but even thinking about not picking his nose made him feel a little queasy.

366. Wes felt pinpricks of heat all over his body.

367. Wes started to shiver and his hands were cold and clammy, even though it was warm inside.

Appearance

368. Wes pinched his eyes shut and sealed his lips as he staggered towards the door.

369. Wes' eyes started to water and his face went green; it was only a matter of time.

370. He couldn't look away; he stared at the snotty-nosed kid like he was a giant cockroach.

371. Wes grimaced and shut his eyes tightly—this was not something he could bear to look at any longer.

372. Wes twisted his mouth into a knot and squinted through his slitted eyes.

373. Wes closed his eyes and bit the inside of his cheek in an effort to distract himself.

Actions

374. He looked over at the car next to him; the driver was digging in his nose. When the light changed, Wes had to pull over and pace around in the fresh air for a few minutes.

375. The meeting had been going so well, but then she scratched the edge of her nostril. Wes stumbled away from the table, mumbling something about the bathroom.

376. Wes knew that this wasn't the time—it was a really important job interview—but he couldn't help it. As the second the man's finger went towards his face, he stood up and rushed for the hallway.

377. Wes doubled over and clenched his stomach like his appendix had just burst.

378. Wes told the disgusting cashier to keep the change and jogged out to the parking lot with one hand over his mouth.

379. Wes moaned and reached for the sick bag; at least throwing up was acceptable on airplanes.

380. Wes smacked his brother's hand away from his face before he even realized he was doing it.

CHAPTER FIVE

Fear

One of the most universal and powerful human emotions is fear. Fear is the belief that something or someone is dangerous or likely to cause you pain. People can experience fear for their physical safety, for their social position, or for their emotional well-being.

This versatile feeling can present itself in many different ways, and all of them can be useful for storytelling.

It is essential that every writer learns how to properly utilize fear in their stories. A fearful character will react in abnormal ways, either because they want to reduce the amount of fear that they are feeling, or because they are so overcome by the emotion that they don't think that they will ever feel normal again.

If a character's fear is portrayed effectively enough, readers will become afraid, too.

Manipulating your readers' emotions in this way will definitely make them want to keep reading, because it will heighten the suspense that drives your story; your audience will become desperate to find out whether your character will rise to the challenge and overcome their fear, or be crushed under its burden.

The following chapter will give overviews of some of the different types of fear that you can use in your writing, and give examples of scenarios and sentences that illustrate the emotion effectively. Once you've finished it, you'll be able to scare any reader out of their wits!

Alienation

One type of fear that can be very fruitful in fiction is alienation. An alienated character feels like he or she is isolated or estranged from those around them.

A character that is experiencing alienation may withdraw themselves from society, fall into a depression, or lash out against the characters they feel are excluding them.

Alienation can be a very powerful tool for writers because characters that feel this way tend to be very introverted. This gives the writer the opportunity to really get inside of their heads and attempt to show what it is like to feel like an outsider.

Here is a basic example of an alienated character: Tasha has recently moved to a new country, but she doesn't speak the language yet. Since she cannot communicate with anyone, she feels alienated from society.

Surroundings

381. Tasha felt like she was walking through a strange dream; everywhere she went, people were laughing and chatting, but she couldn't understand a word of it.

382. Tasha stuck out like a sore thumb; everyone would turn whenever she entered a room.

383. The landscape of the city felt cold and harsh without a single friendly face in sight.

384. Tasha was quite intelligent, but being forced to communicate using gestures and symbols made her feel stupid and small.

385. Nothing here was familiar, nothing was commonplace; she missed home.

386. Tasha wished that she could find just one person here who she could talk to, but nobody ever appeared.

387. Even the birds in the trees seemed to look at her sideways, as if to say, "you don't belong here."

Appearance

388. Tasha's eyes were dull and vacant, as if she looked at everything but didn't actually see anything.

389. Tasha soon forgot how to smile; her mouth stayed in its neutral resting place and her throat grew sore from disuse.

390. Tasha tried to communicate by waggling her eyebrows and grinning, but even these gestures seemed to be lost on the locals, so she gave up.

391. Dark circles sprouted under her eyes, since she hadn't had a peaceful night's sleep in weeks.

392. Tasha's eyes were permanently red from crying about her long lost homeland.

393. Whenever strangers would point questioningly at her, Tasha would bite her lip and keep walking.

Actions

394. At first, Tasha tried to wave at the people she passed on the street, but the gesture didn't seem to translate correctly.

395. Tasha would scribble her thoughts into her notebook when she felt lonely—which was nearly always. It was the only thing that kept her sane.

396. Eventually, Tasha started talking to herself, just to remind herself that she still knew how to do it.

397. When Tasha tripped and fell on the uneven sidewalk, nobody came to her aid.

398. Soon, Tasha started pushing past people without apologizing; if they didn't care about her, why should she care about them?

399. Sometimes, Tasha would peer through the windows of houses at night, watching happy families eat their dinners together.

400. Occasionally, Tasha would pinch her arm until it was raw and red, to remind herself that she was still human.

Fright

One of the most simple feelings of fear is fright.

When a character is frightened, he or she feels afraid and anxious. Something that has happened or is happening to them has made them question their safety and security.

A frightened character may panic, overreacting to a benign situation, or their fear may be perfectly justified. Readers will always be interested in frightened characters, because they will want to determine whether or not the character should be afraid.

If you can illustrate this emotion well enough, you may make the reader afraid themselves, even if though they are in the safety of their own homes. This is a very powerful weapon for any writer, and you should learn how to wield it effectively.

Let's look at a basic example of a frightened character.

Paul is frightened because his car has broken down in a remote area in the middle of the night. He needs to walk a great distance to find help, and on the way his imagination gets the better of him. Every person and shadow that he passes seems like a real and legitimate threat, even though he knows that there is probably nothing to be afraid of.

Surroundings

401. Paul started the long walk back to the last gas station he had passed. Every tree moving in the breeze seemed poised to attack him.

402. The shadows cast by the occasional streetlight looked like assassins hiding on the side of the road, waiting for someone defenseless to walk by.

403. Paul could see a couple of pairs of moonlit eyes off in the distance. He almost screamed, then realized that they belonged to a family of deer.

404. The moon was bright, but the stars were covered by clouds, making the journey even more treacherous.

405. Paul must have been the only one awake for miles in any direction; somehow, this information didn't make him feel any better.

406. A gust of wind blasted down the road, cutting through the warmth of Paul's coat.

407. Paul had a spooky intuition that he was being followed.

Appearance

408. Paul's teeth started to chatter, even though it wasn't particularly cold out.

409. Paul's eyes darted from side to side, tracking any possible movement, looking for anyone waiting to do him harm.

410. Tears began running down Paul's cheeks; he had never felt this helpless before.

411. Paul squinted into the darkness, hoping to see the gas station ahead. There was nothing there.

412. Paul chewed on his bottom lip, a nervous tic that he had developed as a child.

413. Paul frowned and narrowed his eyes, hoping to look as intimidating as possible.

Actions

414. Paul knew that there was nothing to be afraid of, but that didn't stop him from jumping at the sound of every snapping branch in the woods.

415. Paul could feel his heart beating in his chest, and it only made him more nervous. He started to walk even faster.

416. Paul clenched his fists inside of his coat pockets, ready to swing at an attacker at any moment.

417. Paul dialed the number for the police on his telephone, to have it ready just in case. Of course, he didn't have any cell service, which just made him feel even less safe.

418. Paul thought he heard someone coming up from behind him, and broke into a run.

419. Paul tripped over a branch that he couldn't see in the darkness, and shouted.

420. Paul would have given away his life savings for a flashlight, or a baseball bat, but when he searched his car, he found nothing useful.

Inadequacy

Another type of fear that characters can exhibit is inadequacy. A character feels inadequate if they think that they are lacking in ability or usefulness in a situation.

This feeling can lead to frustration and depression, and make characters do things that they ordinarily wouldn't in order to compensate. Inadequacy is a very important emotion for writers to master, because they can use it to move scenes in unexpected directions, which will increase reader interest.

Here is a simple example of inadequacy that will help you understand how to portray this important feeling in your own work. Vanessa was always the best soccer player in her school, until Jamie, a new student, transferred into her class. Jamie is much better at the sport than she is, and so she feels inadequate, even though she is still the second best soccer player in the entire school.

Surroundings

421. She used to feel more comfortable on the pitch than anywhere else in town; now it felt like she had forgotten how to walk the second she stepped out onto the grass.

422. All eyes were on Jamie; nobody even passed Vanessa the ball for what seemed like hours.

423. Even when she practiced at home, it seemed like the ball just wouldn't do what she wanted it to.

424. Soccer was the source of her confidence, and now that confidence had been shaken. She started mumbling in class and tripping over her shoelaces in the hallway.

425. Her coach always gave her a little extra attention at practice, but today, he didn't even say hello.

426. Vanessa wished that she had never seen a soccer ball; she wished that soccer had never even been invented.

427. She used to feel like a star when she walked around downtown. Now she felt like a nobody.

Appearance

428. Vanessa stared down at her feet and sighed.

429. Vanessa winced whenever Jamie scored a goal.

430. Vanessa scrunched up her eyes and moaned like she had a stomach ache.

431. Vanessa blinked back the tears and gave a weak smile; she couldn't cry, not in front of Jamie.

432. Vanessa bit her lip so hard that it started to bleed.

433. Vanessa stared ahead blankly, like she wasn't really looking at anything.

Actions

434. Vanessa kicked at a rock angrily, but she missed it and her leg just flew into the air.

435. Vanessa stuffed her hands into her pockets and walked quickly down the sidewalk, hoping that Jamie wouldn't see her.

436. Vanessa let the air out of all of her soccer balls and threw her cleats into the trash.

437. Vanessa kicked her ball against the garage door over and over again, until the sun went down, but she still didn't feel like she had improved.

438. Vanessa sank down to her knees and buried her face in her hands.

439. Vanessa flung her hands above her head and groaned.

440. Vanessa spat on the ground in between them, aiming for Jamie's shoes, but she couldn't even do that accurately.

Overwhelm

Another type of fear that comes from a character's environment is the feeling of being overwhelmed. Someone is overwhelmed when they feel like they have committed to too many things, which makes them stressed out and panicky.

Once a character is overwhelmed, they may not be able to complete the simplest of tasks, because they are too concerned with all of the other things that they have to do.

This is a very powerful tool for writers, because an overwhelmed character can make a lot of simple mistakes that they otherwise would not have, which adds additional obstacles between them and their goals, complicating any situation and making it more interesting.

Here is a classic example of being overwhelmed that any student can relate to. John has waited until the last minute to study for his finals, and now they are only two days away. He doesn't have enough time to prepare for his classes effectively, which sends him into a spiral of panic and despair.

Surroundings

441. The world felt like it was closing in on him; everything was piling up on all sides.

442. John stayed up until midnight surrounded by his notes, but he was too distracted by his impending doom to actually look at them.

443. It would have taken only two minutes for John to brush his teeth, but he didn't have time; he didn't have time for anything.

444. John felt like all of his teachers were jeering at him, hoping that he would fail.

445. John looked at the test in front of him. The letters began to wobble and dance around the page; he couldn't make sense of them.

446. John was so far behind already that even the thought of opening his science textbook made him queasy.

447. John knew that he needed to focus now more than ever, but he felt like the cartoon on the TV was the only thing keeping him from losing his mind completely.

Appearance

448. John had deep, dark bags under his eyes; he hadn't slept for more than four hours a night all week.

449. John could feel his nose twitching, but he couldn't do anything to stop it.

450. Droplets of sweat started to cluster on John's forehead and his breath quickened—he wasn't sure if he could even turn the page now.

451. John gritted his teeth and furrowed his brow, hoping to force himself to concentrate.

452. John raised his eyebrows way up on his forehead and blinked slowly, like his eyes were cameras and he needed to take a picture of every page.

453. John frowned and squinted at the sentence, reading it over and over, but it still made absolutely no sense.

Actions

454. John ran to the bathroom and splashed ice cold water on his face, then slapped himself on the cheek to try to wake up.

455. John never really drank coffee before, but he finished two whole pots of the nasty stuff before the night was through.

456. John began pacing back and forth around the living room like a crazy person; somehow, the movement helped him think a little more clearly.

457. John threw his notebook across the room in frustration; it landed on the ground like a crumpled accordion of gibberish.

458. John almost stood up and walked out of the classroom; he was going to fail anyway, what was the point of even trying?

459. At dinner, John just moved his food around the plate without eating anything; hunger was the last thing on his mind.

460. John's hands were shaking; he couldn't even read his own handwriting.

Worry

One very common type of fear is worry. A person becomes worried when they are preoccupied with a situation that they think will end badly for them. This feeling may cause characters to obsess over their problems, behave irrationally, or fall into a depression.

Worry is a useful addition to any writer's arsenal, because when a character is worried, he or she will consider their predicament over and over again, which allows the writer to show the situation from many different angles.

Here is a basic example of a worried character that you can use as a model for your own stories: Jeff's friend, Doug, has been acting strange towards him lately. He has been cold and distant when they spend time together, and has cancelled several of their plans over the last few weeks. Jeff is worried about Doug and his behavior.

Surroundings

461. Nothing could make Jeff happy these days. He couldn't even laugh at his favorite movies.

462. Whenever he had the chance to actually hang out with Doug, Jeff felt like a pane of glass was separating them.

463. Jeff walked home in the pouring rain, and felt a little better; at least the weather was matching his mood.

464. Doug probably left his phone on his table by mistake, but Jeff took it as more irrefutable proof that he was up to something more sinister.

465. He even managed to twist unlucky coincidences that had nothing to do with him into evidence of the bad news to come.

466. Jeff knew it wasn't helping, but whenever Doug so much as sighed he made sure to ask him what was wrong.

467. When Doug cancelled their fishing trip yet again, Jeff snuck over to his house to make sure that he wasn't up to any suspicious business.

Appearance

468. Jeff looked like he hadn't slept in days, never mind taken a shower.

469. Jeff's eyes were bloodshot from crying into his pillows.

470. Jeff stared at Doug a little too intensely, hoping to catch signs of his discontent as soon as they appeared.

471. When Jeff smiled, Doug could see that his teeth were coated with a thick layer of plaque; he'd been too obsessed with their problems to remember to brush that morning.

472. Jeff stared at Doug hopelessly; he looked like he might cry at any moment.

473. Jeff looked sick; his skin was yellowish and he seemed to have lost ten pounds overnight.

Actions

474. Jeff brushed the tear from his eye, pretending that a lash had gotten stuck under his eyelid.

475. Jeff took long walks late into the night, wondering when Doug would just put him out of his misery.

476. Jeff started collecting the things that Doug had left in his apartment in a cardboard box, certain that he would come for them sooner or later.

477. Jeff chewed his fingernails down to stumps.

478. Jeff started to pull at a loose string in his sleeve to distract himself. Before long, his whole shirt was frayed and he had to throw it out.

479. Jeff started to follow Doug in his car. He knew that Doug would no longer trust him the second he caught him doing it, but Jeff was desperate to learn the truth.

480. Jeff couldn't remember the last time he had eaten a proper meal; he was too concerned about Doug to keep himself well fed.

Worthlessness

The last type of fear that we will discuss is worthlessness. A character feels worthless when they believe that they have no redeeming qualities left. This usually happens as a reaction to a huge failure of some kind, or a tragedy.

When a character feels worthless, they can fall into a deep depression and behave in abnormal, unpredictable, and self-destructive ways. This can be a fantastic emotion to harness for use in your own work, because characters who feel worthless often generate a lot of sympathy from readers, and behave in surprising ways that can bring stories to completely unexpected places.

Here is an example of a character who feels worthless.

Tessa has already lost her family, her boyfriend, and her cat, all in the same month. Dealing with all of these events has totally drained her energy, which means that she has been slacking off at work. Today, she has been fired from her job—the only thing she had left to keep her sane—because of her lack of motivation. If she doesn't find some way to make money soon, she will be living on the street. All of these things, combined, make her feel worthless, as if she is the root cause of everything bad that has happened to her.

Surroundings

481. The whole party seemed dull and glum; Tessa was sure that if she wasn't here, everybody would be having a better time.

482. She passed by a pet shop. She wanted to buy herself a new cat, but even if she had the money, she knew that the cat would be better off as somebody else's pet.

483. There was a help wanted sign in the window, but Tessa didn't have the energy to bother going in to ask for an application. Besides, who would want a girl like her to work for them, anyway?

484. People bumped into her on the sidewalk, pushing by without any kind of apology. She didn't blame them.

485. Tessa sat near her parents' gravestone, a little envious that they didn't have to deal with this cruel planet any longer.

486. It was a beautiful day, but Tessa stayed inside with her blinds drawn. She didn't deserve to feel the warmth of the sun on her neck.

487. Tessa had an umbrella in her purse, but she didn't pull it out. She might as well get soaked with rain; it didn't make any difference.

Appearance

488. Tessa looked so drained and hopeless that a man dropped a quarter into her coffee cup as he passed her on the street.

489. Tessa stared at nothing at all, ignoring the strange looks that people gave her when they accidentally made eye contact.

490. Tessa looked like a ghost; if you held a light up to her face, you could see right through her.

491. Tessa wanted to smile at the little girl who skipped past her, but she had forgotten how to do it, so it came across as more of a wince.

492. Long strands of hair had matted themselves across Tessa's face, but she didn't have the energy to move them.

493. Tessa sat slumped in the corner; she went so long without blinking that the man thought she may have fallen asleep with her eyes open.

Actions

494. Tessa walked across the busy street without waiting for the light to change; cars honked and swerved to avoid hitting her.

495. Tessa held her hand over the candle until it burned, but she didn't really feel anything.

496. Tessa hung out in the bank lobby and thought about robbing the place. After a while, she realized that she didn't even know what she would do with all the money, so she just left.

497. Tessa fell asleep on her couch with her front door wide open. She lived in a pretty dangerous neighborhood, but she didn't think that anything could happen to make her feel any worse than she already did.

498. Tessa hadn't done her laundry in weeks. She grabbed a pair of dirty socks off the floor and put them on her feet inside-out.

499. Tessa yawned as the mugger demanded her wallet. He was so shocked that he asked her if she was okay. She laughed for the first time in months.

500. Tessa stood on top of a hill during a thunderstorm, hoping that she would get struck by lightning.

CHAPTER SIX

Happiness

Another key emotion that everyone has experienced is happiness. Happiness is a state of well-being characterized by pleasure, satisfaction, contentment, and joy.

People can be happy because their plans are finally working out, because good things are happening to them and those around them, or simply because they've walked outside into beautiful weather. As you can see, this feeling presents itself in many different ways, with many different levels of intensity, all of which can have specific effects on your audience.

One of the best skills that a writer can develop is the ability to successfully portray happiness in their work. Just like real people, the basic goal of almost any well-developed character is to become happy. Once this happens —usually towards the end of a story—all of the hardship and stress that has weighed down on the character will suddenly lift, and everything that they've gone through will seem like it was worth it.

When writers properly illustrate this change in feeling, their readers will experience happiness of their own, resulting in a real emotional release that goes a long way towards making any story great.

Since happiness is such a basic and universal idea, it can sometimes be hard for new writers to properly get the emotion across to their readers on paper. In the following chapter, we offer a simple solution to this problem: like everything else that you've learned about emotions so far, the more specific and detailed a description is, the better.

We have picked out some of the most important forms of happiness, and given some examples of ways that you can harness their power in your own work. By deciding exactly which form of happiness your characters are experiencing, and using the language that is most suited to those emotions, you'll be making readers smile to themselves in no time!

Amusement

One of the more mild forms of happiness is amusement. A character becomes amused when they experience something that they find humorous, funny, or entertaining.

Amusement can go a long way to making readers feel sympathetic towards your main characters—but it's important to remember that likable characters are not the only ones who can feel amused. If something terrible and tragic happens in front of your villain, and he begins cackling with glee, this form of amusement will make the readers hate him even more, which can be very useful indeed.

Here is a simple example of an amused character that you can use as a model for your own work: Jeremy is attending a concert played by The Emotions, his all-time-favorite band. He's listened to The Emotions for years, owns all of their records, but this is the first time that he's been able to see them in person.

Surroundings

501. The room was packed with people; they weren't dancing as much as swaying as a group, but nobody seemed to mind.

502. Everything that was going on in school and at home, all of Jeremy's problems, faded away in an instant. All that was left was the music.

503. When the set was over, a complete stranger gave Jeremy a hug. He felt like he had known her for years.

504. Johnny Smiles, the lead singer of The Emotions, cracked a few jokes on stage. The entire crowd doubled over with laughter.

505. When Jeremy left the venue, his ears were ringing, he felt like he could fall asleep standing up, and he was happy.

506. When the band took a bow and walked offstage, everyone hollered and cheered, begging for an encore.

507. Rainbow colored confetti started falling from the sky and at every corner, a new surprise awaited.

Appearance

508. Jeremy grinned from ear to ear when The Emotions stepped onstage.

509. Jeremy's eyes were bright and focused. He didn't even want to blink; he didn't want to miss anything.

510. Jeremy felt tears come to his eyes. He couldn't handle the sheer wonder of it all.

511. Jeremy smiled and leaned his head way back with his eyes closed, letting the music wash over him.

512. Jeremy's hair was matted to his forehead, and sweat glistened all over his body, but he just laughed when he saw his crush in the merchandise line; this was no time to feel self-conscious.

513. Jeremy looked forward with an unfocused gaze and a dropped jaw; he looked like he was being hypnotized.

Actions

514. People kept stepping on Jeremy's toes, but he couldn't care less.

515. Jeremy whooped and shouted and sang along until his throat ached and his voice was hoarse.

516. Jeremy climbed up on his friend's shoulders and launched himself out into the crowd, surfing on top of the masses.

517. Jeremy was dancing like a total idiot, but he didn't care what anyone else thought.

518. Jeremy couldn't stop shaking his head and laughing; he couldn't believe he was here.

519. Jeremy tried to climb on stage, but the security guards stopped him. He shrugged his shoulders and walked away, humming to himself.

520. Jeremy took a break and leaned against the wall, watching the people dance and jump all around him as he smiled.

Ecstasy

One of the most intense versions of happiness is ecstasy. A character feels ecstatic when they are overwhelmed by joy and excitement. They may become giddy, hyperactive, or silly, and basically act like children at a carnival, regardless of their normal demeanor.

Almost nothing can bring a truly ecstatic character down: today is the best day of their life.

Successfully illustrating ecstasy can be difficult, but if it is done correctly, it can evoke very strong reactions on the part of the reader. Ecstatic characters are very helpful in comedic situations, because their over-the-top behavior tends to add to the ridiculousness. If you really want to make your readers laugh, bringing an ecstatic character into the mix is a sure-fire way to do it!

Here is a situation involving an ecstatic character: Jenna has just won a raffle at a local fair. The winnings are only fifty dollars, but she has never won anything before, so she feels like a millionaire.

Surroundings

521. Suddenly the sun was shining, the grass was greener, and everyone around Jenna looked beautiful and perfect.

522. Jenna was sure that any second now, the crowd would lift her off her feet and carry her around the room on their shoulders.

523. Jenna peered down at her ticket. She was so excited that her vision blurred; two sets of winning numbers weaved in and out of one another.

524. On the outside, Jenna looked calm, but it took every ounce of her self-control to keep from sprinting up to the stage and tackling the announcer with a bear hug.

525. Jenna was handed five of the crispest, cleanest ten dollar bills she had ever seen in her life.

526. She must have been going crazy; Jenna thought she heard a swing band with a full horn section celebrating her good fortune.

527. Jenna knew that she was making a fool of herself by acting so giddy, but she didn't care.

Appearance

528. Jenna's eyes widened and her jaw dropped halfway to the floor.

529. Jenna beamed for so long that she could feel her cheeks starting to ache.

530. Jenna's eyebrows were raised so high that she wondered if they would ever come back down again.

531. Jenna's eyes darted back and forth; she wanted to take in the whole scene, to remember exactly what was happening when she won.

532. Tears of happiness streamed down her face, but she was too excited to notice them.

533. Jenna was so full of adrenaline that she couldn't remember the last time she blinked.

Actions

534. Jenna threw her hands above her head and squealed.

535. Jenna began to dance in a tight circle, like she was an athlete showboating after she scored a point.

536. Jenna's hands were shaking as she reached out to claim her winnings.

537. Jenna wrapped her arms around herself tightly, as if she wanted to trap the good feelings inside of her for as long as possible.

538. Jenna knew that she was being silly, but she went around the stage shaking everybody's hands and thanking them profusely.

539. For hours afterwards, Jenna could not sit still. She paced around her house in frantic circles well into the night.

540. It was in times like these that Jenna wished she could do a backflip; she contented herself with a polite bow towards the fair-goers.

Fulfillment

Another form of happiness is fulfillment. A character feels fulfilled when he or she has finally achieved something that they have desired or been promised for a very long time.

While it manifests itself in more subtle ways than the craziness brought on from ecstasy, genuine fulfillment is one of the most lasting and powerful types of happiness that one can aspire to, because it represents overcoming a true challenge successfully.

Similarly to contentment, fulfillment is often used near the end of stories. Once a character has gained what they were looking for the entire time, they can feel like their life finally has meaning, or like good things will continue to happen to them. This is quite useful, because it allows the character to become a little introspective and look back on the journey that they have taken. The reader will follow this line of thinking, and the general point of the story will be highlighted for them a little more clearly.

Ending stories with the fulfillment of your characters is an easy way to get in a "message" that might have seemed a bit cheesy if you came right out and said it, especially in the beginning or middle of your story.

Here is an example of a fulfilled character: Billy has spent thirty years sending letters to his mother who lives overseas, even though she has never responded once. The mother— a woman named Grace—has traveled across the world to his doorstep, and now they are catching up.

Surroundings

541. There she was, sitting across the table from him. The usually harsh light of Billy's kitchen took on a warm, rosy glow.

542. Billy felt like a massive weight had been lifted off of his chest; he felt like he could die right now and that would be okay.

543. Everything he had been hoping and dreaming for, every fantasy of his long and dull life, was coming true.

544. There were sparrows chirping in the garden, providing the perfect soundtrack to the idyllic scene.

545. His mother looked more beautiful than ever; it was as if an angel was standing before him, hovering just above the ground.

546. For weeks, Billy just laughed at every little inconvenience that normally would have ruined his day. *Who cares?* he thought, *I have everything I've ever wanted now.*

547. Billy was never a creative man, but he wanted to paint his mother's portrait, or to write her a sonnet; he wanted to do something to show that she had finally made the right decision.

Appearance

548. Billy's eyes were lidded and heavy, and a slow smile crept across his face.

549. For days, Billy found himself grinning for no reason, even in the shower.

550. The dark bags under Billy's eyes vanished overnight; there was nothing left to keep him from sleeping soundly.

551. Billy's skin looked clearer, and he seemed to glow from within.

552. Billy closed his eyes and took a deep breath, savoring the contentment.

553. Billy was a tough guy, but every time his mother said something sweet to him, he'd blush like a schoolgirl.

Actions

554. Billy leaned back in his recliner with his hands folded behind his head, as if he'd just eaten a filling meal.

555. He would often look up into the sky and smile, thanking the universe for letting him have what he'd always wanted.

556. Billy even became more productive around the house; the time that he used to spend pining for contact with his mother was now filled with weeding the garden and cleaning out the garage.

557. Billy started to help the elderly woman who lived across the street with her yard work, too; he felt like he needed to give something back, to share the happiness that he'd found.

558. Billy made his mother a little wooden rabbit that he'd whittled from a block of pine; it was the best that he could do to show her that he cared.

559. Billy started to hold doors open for people, and to let faster cars pass him on the highway without laying on his horn.

560. When he first saw his mother on his front porch; Billy dropped to his knees with tears in his eyes and laughed.

Liberation

Liberation is one of the most interesting and valuable forms of happiness. A character feels liberated when they are released from oppression, imprisonment, or a heavy burden. This emotion is characterized by a profound feeling of relief and positivity. The one thing that has been keeping a character from happiness has been overcome, and now they feel like the possibilities are endless.

Much like fulfillment, liberation is most effectively used by writers near the ends of their stories. If a character has been tormented by a villain or a terrible situation, liberation sets in once they have won the battle against their foe. They may do or say things that previously wouldn't have been possible for them, or simply feel grateful that the whole ordeal is over.

By allowing your characters to feel liberated, you will signal to your readers that the struggle they've been following so closely is over, and the protagonist has come out on top. If you do this correctly, your audience will feel relieved that their favorite character can begin to live a happier and more normal life.

Let's take a look at a specific example of liberation, which you can use as a template for your own stories: Michelle was wrongfully convicted for the murder of her best friend, Anthony. She has been in jail for most of the story. Now, because of the hard work of her friends and family, the real killer has been caught and she is free.

Surroundings

561. For weeks, Michelle would stare out of car windows, marveling at the vast fields that stretched away from the roads for miles; she hadn't been able to observe sheer space like that for a long time.

562. It was late fall, and getting chilly, but Michelle spent as much time as she could outdoors, feeling the sun on her skin and breathing in the fresh air.

563. Michelle hung around downtown, catching up with her old friends and even her enemies; she was just glad to have somebody to talk to.

564. After the whole ordeal, Michelle realized that her life was pretty much perfect. All of the stupid things that used to worry her so much seemed silly, once she put them in perspective.

565. Michelle took a long hike to the top of a nearby mountain; her legs ached when she finally reached the summit, but she had never felt so free.

566. Michelle would sometimes have dreams that she was still in prison; she'd wake up in a cold sweat, then begin to laugh, because it was all over.

567. Michelle had trouble adjusting to the idea that she could go wherever she wanted; she kept looking around for somebody to give her permission.

Appearance

568. Michelle let out a sigh, then smiled with her eyes closed.

569. Michelle's eyes darted back and forth, eager to absorb the whole scene in front of her.

570. Michelle looked well-rested and healthy; her skin was bright and her eyes had a flash of alertness in them that wasn't there before.

571. When Michelle spotted a friend who clearly hadn't heard that she'd been released, she grinned and waggled her eyebrows.

572. Michelle yawned luxuriously and smacked her lips together, basking in the comfort of an afternoon nap.

573. When Michelle finally saw her mother, her vision was blurred by her tears, but she couldn't stop smiling.

Actions

574. The first night that she got out, Michelle wrapped herself in a blanket and sat on the front porch with a thermos full of coffee. When the sun rose, she started to cry; she'd never seen anything quite so beautiful.

575. Michelle started to write letters to defense attorneys on behalf of wrongfully convicted people throughout the country; she felt like she needed to do something to help, now that she was on the outside.

576. Michelle began waking up earlier in the mornings. She'd been given a second chance, and she wasn't going to waste it by hanging around and being lazy.

577. Michelle donated a lot of her clothing and knickknacks to charity; she'd learned that she didn't need all of these possessions to be happy.

578. Michelle ran around with her dog in the backyard for what felt like hours; it felt good to be sore and out of breath.

579. Michelle decided to take a long road trip across the country, just to flex her wings a little and remind herself of what it meant to be free.

580. Michelle spent the entire day watching TV in her pajamas, just because she could.

Love

One form of happiness that everyone is familiar with is love.

A character feels love towards another character that they have a lot of care and affection for. This is a deep and powerful bond, stronger than almost every other emotion.

If a character loves someone, they will do whatever it takes to make sure that that person is happy and safe. They will risk their own safety and security in order to meet the needs of the person they love. This feeling is sometimes reciprocated by the other character, sometimes not, but it makes for a very interesting story either way!

At a basic level, love is one of the most common and influential themes in literature. Even stories that aren't directly about love usually involve it in some way, like friendship or a close familial bond.

As such, it is essential that any writer master the portrayal of this emotion.

Characters can fall in love slowly, or instantly, but there are always verbal and physical clues that writers can use to show their audience that love is in the air. With a little practice, you'll be able to capture this emotion perfectly. It's definitely worth the effort; everyone likes a good love story!

Here is an example of love that you can use in your own work: Walter is falling in love with his coworker, Christine, but he isn't sure if she feels the same way about him. (Spoiler Alert: she does!)

Surroundings

581. Whenever Christine walked into the room, it seemed like everything moved in slow motion.

582. Walter was in a predicament; he wanted to impress Christine with his work ethic, but he couldn't seem to accomplish anything when she was nearby.

583. On Tuesday, Christine was unable to come into work. Walter spent his whole shift in a state of despair; it felt like the day would never end.

584. Every once in a while, Walter would catch Christine looking at him from across the room. She would look away whenever they made eye contact.

585. Christine and Walter started taking their lunch breaks together. He told himself that she was just being friendly, but she never ate with any of their other coworkers.

586. Walter's heart would skip a beat whenever he saw Christine's name on the weekly schedule.

587. Walter offered to walk Christine home. It was freezing cold outside, but he was too nervous to even notice.

Appearance

588. Christine was looking at him with a quizzical expression on her face; it took him five seconds to realize that he was staring at her with his mouth wide open.

589. Christine blushed and messed with her hair when Walter told her that she looked pretty in her new dress.

590. Walter's face flushed and his mouth went dry; he'd never work up the courage to ask her out.

591. When Christine agreed to go on a date with him, Walter didn't stop smiling for hours.

592. Christine swooped in and gave Walter a peck on the cheek. His jaw dropped and his eyes went wide; it looked like someone had just dumped a bucket of cold water on his head.

593. As Walter saw Christine approaching down the hallway; a smile crept across his face, and all of the tension he was feeling evaporated.

Actions

594. Christine borrowed Walter's sweatshirt one afternoon. When she gave it back, the hood smelled like her shampoo. After that, he wore it constantly for a week.

595. Walter was too busy staring at Christine to realize that the cup he was filling was overflowing onto the table.

596. Walter's hands were shaking as he reached over to intertwine his fingers with hers.

597. When they kissed, it felt like Walter was being struck by lightning. The whole world faded away, she was the only thing that mattered.

598. Walter made Christine a mixed CD of his favorite songs. He spent twelve hours picking them out, because he wanted to make sure that it was perfect.

599. Walter started to write Christine's name down over and over in the margins of his notebook.

600. Walter made sure to laugh at all of Christine's jokes, even the stupid ones.

Playfulness

Another type of happiness is playfulness. A playful character is lighthearted, fond of games and amusement. They don't tend to take things too seriously, preferring instead to have as much fun as possible.

Playful characters are very likable, and often serve as a source of comic relief, especially in more serious stories.

Playfulness is a great emotion for any writer to add to their arsenal. It is very important to include a few sympathetic characters in your stories, people that your audience can identify with and root for. Playful characters fill this role perfectly; it's really hard not to like someone who doesn't take themselves too seriously.

If you create a character that isn't afraid to joke around and have fun, your audience will like them automatically, which will buy you a lot of essential reader attention.

Remember, your ultimate goal is to make people read your stories all the way to the end; if you can get them laughing along with your characters, you've already won half the battle!

Let's take a look at an example of playfulness that you can model your own characters on: Kara and Frank are on vacation in a foreign city. They are hopelessly lost, and don't speak the language. Frank, who is very serious, is panicking, but Kara's playful nature allows her to enjoy herself, even in a stressful situation.

Surroundings

601. People were passing them on all sides, on their way to work. Frank was starting to freak out, but the craziness of the crowds made Kara even more excited.

602. They were in a foreign country, in a strange city, and they had no idea where they were or where they were headed. Finally, Kara thought, a real adventure.

603. It started to rain, which made Frank grumble even more. Kara thought that it made the city look even more mysterious and wonderful.

604. Kara saw the world through rose-colored glasses. Everywhere she looked was full of excitement, opportunity, and friendship.

605. Even though the pedestrians looked bored and glum—they were just going about their normal business—Kara felt like she was in the middle of a carnival.

606. Kara wished that she could stay lost forever, running around a weird city, living in the now.

607. Kara sat on a bench in the middle of the square, patiently waiting for more chaos to appear.

Appearance

608. Kara, desperate not to miss a thing, went so long between blinks that Frank started wondering if she was in a trance.

609. Kara grinned from ear to ear and raised an eyebrow, begging Frank to let her go into one more shop before they headed out to the main street.

610. Kara stared at the street performers with an open mouth and widened eyes; she'd never seen anyone juggling flaming swords before.

611. Kara doubled over and laughed so hard that it looked like it hurt; her face went beet red, and there were tears in the corners of her eyes.

612. Kara winked at Frank and gave him a half smile, then went to make friends with the cashier.

613. Kara batted her eyelashes and smiled so wide that Frank could see all of her teeth.

Actions

614. Kara tore Frank's map into two pieces and handed the bottom half back to him, explaining that this would make navigation more challenging and fun.

615. Frank wanted to retrace their steps and find the main road, but Kara kept ducking into stores whenever a whimsical object caught her eye.

616. Kara saw a bunch of cute little kids playing hopscotch in a parking lot. Frank had to hold her back to keep her from trying to jump in and play with them.

617. Kara's head swiveled around; she'd gawk at the most interesting thing she could see for a while, then switch targets when she started getting bored.

618. Kara skipped off and tried to ask somebody for directions using only hand signals.

619. Frank was only halfway through yelling at Kara for being so carefree in a dangerous situation, but she wrapped him in a bearhug and wouldn't let go until he gave up.

620. Kara told Frank to calm down, then jogged over to a stranger and tried to pet their dog.

CHAPTER SEVEN

Mistrust

Mistrust, similar to distrust, is an emotion characterized by a lack of confidence.

It can take on many forms and have various subjects; but most often, its expression is almost always negative because there is often a major deficiency or betrayal of some kind that leads to a loss of confidence and trust.

Mistrust is an interesting emotion to use because there are many ways in fiction to use it. Your character may mistrust their best friend after finding out that their best friend had leaked their secret. Your character could even harbor mistrust towards their sense of touch, after suffering a mind-altering disease that affected their ability to feel.

There's always a backstory to mistrust which makes for an interesting story. Readers will want to know why your characters cannot trust someone or something and whether they will resolve this lack of trust, or whether...the lack of trust will serve them well in helping them avoid future problems!

Sometimes mistrust can be spun around to serve as a positive learning experience so that characters do not repeat the mistakes they once made.

This chapter will discuss many different level of mistrust, some of them intense and other ones comparatively mild. By the end, you should have a pretty good idea of some ways to use this feeling in your own work.

Hesitancy

Hesitancy happens when a character is unsure or tentative about his or her decisions or actions. Other characters may be egging them on to do something that they wouldn't normally do on their own, which creates an internal conflict as they decide whether or not to trust themselves and go through with the plan.

This can be a very effective feeling to use in your stories, because it forces your characters to slow down a little bit and weigh the pros and cons of their actions. This heightens suspense, since the readers will wonder what your character will decide, and will probably root for one of the possible options over the other.

Let's look closely at one scenario where a character experiences hesitancy. Janet is a top student at her school. There is an important math test at the end of the week that is worth more than half of the grade for the semester. Her best friend, Theresa—who sits next to her in class—is terrible at math, and has begged Janet to let her cheat off of her test. Janet spends the entire week trying to decide whether she should help her friend or not.

Surroundings

621. Janet took a long walk by herself, hoping that the universe would give her a sign. She stayed outside until after dark, but nothing seemed to happen.

622. Somehow, everything that happened that week seemed related to the big decision. The people on tv, her parents' dinner conversations, everybody was talking about cheating in one way or another.

623. Janet felt paranoid as she walked through the store with her hands in her pockets. After all, she was considering letting Theresa cheat off of her test; was that really so different from shoplifting?

624. Janet deliberately avoided Theresa all week, worried that she would be caught conspiring with her.

625. At church on Sunday, the priest delivered a sermon on the benefits of honesty and good deeds. Janet left more confused than ever.

626. There was a long line at the movie theater. Janet thought about cutting it, to try out breaking a minor rule, but then she realized that her predicament was different; cutting the line would only be helping herself.

627. The morning of the test, Janet woke up feeling miserable. She considered faking sick, but decided that there was no sense in ruining her own future on top of Theresa's.

Appearance

628. Janet bit her lip and groaned.

629. By the end of the week, Janet had bags under her eyes from lack of sleep.

630. Janet furrowed her brow and frowned, trying to concentrate on the task at hand.

631. Janet closed her eyes and rubbed her temples; all of this thinking had given her a headache.

632. Janet ground her teeth and winced.

633. Janet's eyes shifted back and forth as she weighed her options.

Actions

634. Janet made a list of the pros and cons of letting her friend cheat—she added new points as quickly as she crossed out others but just as she was about to make a decision, she stopped.

635. Janet knew that she should be studying for the test no matter what, but every time she opened her math book, she felt nauseous and had to slam it shut.

636. By Friday morning, Janet had chewed her fingernails down to nubs.

637. As she sat down in front of the test, Janet's hands began to shake uncontrollably.

638. Janet stayed up late into the night, asking her walls if it was better to be honest or help a person in need. They never replied.

639. Janet could feel Theresa's eyes on her; she slid the test towards her, then pulled it back, then slid it towards her again, still unsure about her decision.

640. When her mother asked her how the end of the semester was going, Janet nearly burst into tears, then said "fine" and quickly changed the subject.

Skepticism

Skepticism is a strong form of mistrust, illustrated by doubt. When a character is skeptical, they won't immediately believe the ideas that are being presented to them. This may manifest itself as a lack of enthusiasm, interest, or concern, depending on the context.

Skepticism can be very useful in stories because it can help to show that a character needs to be convinced of something.

This makes the task at hand more difficult for the other characters, which leads to increased conflict and more elaborate conversations. If every character takes what he or she is told at face value, the resulting story will become very short and boring.

By using skepticism effectively, you can make sure that your protagonists don't get what they want too easily, or make them force the other characters to explain their plans more thoroughly before they get involved. Below, we have compiled some examples of skepticism that will help show how important this emotion can be used in fiction.

Surroundings

641. When he stepped out of his car, a twenty dollar bill was lying on the ground in front of him. He looked around for a while before he picked it up, making sure that it wasn't some kind of trap.

642. There was a pamphlet in her mailbox promising to solve all of her problems; she stuck it with the rest of the bills and advertisements.

643. He questioned the salesman for five minutes before agreeing to take a free sample.

644. She knew that the play was boasting free admission, but brought some cash along just in case.

645. The bank manager promised him that there was nothing sinister in the fine print, but he made sure to read through the entire contract anyway.

646. The hospital staff told her that she was free to leave at any time, but she stuck around for a couple of extra days to make sure that none of the other discharged patients were dragged back in against their will.

647. His father gave him the keys to the new car, saying that it was just a simple gift, but he was sure that there were strings attached.

Appearance

648. He narrowed his eyes and asked for more information.

649. She kept her expression as neutral as possible, even though she wanted to smile and shout.

650. She yawned and smoothed out her dress, pretending like she heard offers like this every day.

651. He was agreeing with everything he heard, but slowly shaking his head at the same time.

652. She raised her eyebrows but didn't let herself smile.

653. He blinked slowly, and his eyes glazed over.

Actions

654. She folded her arms and started to inspect her shoes, carefully and actively looking for scuff marks—signs of wear and tear.

655. He moved his hand in a small circle, indicating that he wanted to reach the end of the pitch as quickly as possible.

656. She looked up at the sky for support, hoping that she would be given a sign of what to do.

657. He started to pick the dirt out from beneath his fingernails.

658. She started to check her messages, telling the man that she was still listening.

659. He leaned up against the wall and sighed, certain that he was about to be asked for money.

660. She cracked her knuckles one at a time, then tried to remove the piece of food that was stuck in her teeth with her tongue.

Suspicion

Suspicion is very similar to skepticism, in that it is a form of mistrust. The difference between them is that while a skeptical character can be convinced that their doubt was needless, a suspicious character is almost certain that the situation is not in their best interests.

Suspicious characters believe that they are dealing with someone or something that is dishonest, mistrustful, or sinister. This emotion can be shown in the form of aggression, intense disinterest, or clipped speech and physical reactions.

Suspicion can be a very useful tool for any story because it makes the job of convincing a character to do something much more difficult.

While it is possible for a suspicious character to come around and realize that they are behaving illogically, it is far more likely that they will never change their opinion of the situation at hand.

This makes them a particularly difficult obstacle for a protagonist to overcome, which can lead to the protagonist's plan failing, making it necessary for them to try a different approach to achieve their goals.

If you use suspicion the right way, your stories can become much more complicated and suspenseful, which is always a good thing. Here are some examples of ways that you can use suspicion in your own work:

Surroundings

661. They all stopped talking abruptly when he walked in the room; he knew that he was the subject of their discussion.

662. She was sure that the shopkeeper tried to finish locking up even faster when he saw her walking towards him.

663. The mechanic must have taken one look at his suit and decided to charge him twice as much for the repairs.

664. She wondered if the landlord had refrained from replacing the burnt out bulb in the hallway just to make the building seem spookier.

665. His father knew that he had a fear of germs, but he buried his hand into the candy bowl right before passing it along, just to spite him.

666. There were half a dozen bicycles chained to the fence when she attached hers there, but somehow hers was the only one that was taken.

667. He was certain that his neighbors positioned a huge speaker facing their shared wall, in order to keep him awake as late into the night as possible.

Appearance

668. He scrunched up his eyes and frowned.

669. Her eyes darted around the room, as if an attacker could come from any direction.

670. He pursed his lips and said nothing.

671. She could feel her nostrils flaring—an involuntary tic that happened whenever she thought she was being taken advantage of—but couldn't do anything to stop it.

672. He furrowed his brow and gritted his teeth.

673. She set her jaw at an angle and bit her lip.

Actions

674. He balled up his rival's apology letter and threw it over his shoulder— he knew it couldn't be genuine.

675. She clutched her purse strap reflexively, even though there was no chance that he would lunge across his desk and grab for it.

676. Every evening, as soon as his mother left for work, John quickly slipped on his gloves and slowly examined every report filed in her cabinet. He was sure that he would find something incriminating soon.

677. She stood behind the curtains and, without making a noise, steadied her recording camera into position, ready to capture the culprit.

678. From the attic, he was like a hawk, watching his friend's every move. As his friend turned his head towards his direction, he ducked behind the curtains in an effort to stay invisible.

679. She marched through to the kitchen cupboard, swung open the door and swiped her finger on the white dust. Her instincts were right, someone was there just moments ago!

680. Now was the chance for Ron to get the evidence he needed—in a matter of 60 minutes, he had downloaded 15 years worth of data from Pam's computer and disappeared into the darkness with the drive tucked safely under his arm.

CHAPTER EIGHT

Pride

A complex and interesting emotion is pride—when it is seen in a positive light, pride refers to someone who is fulfilled and content, yet also humble. However, when seen in a negative light, pride be the source of ridicule and self-righteousness as characters possess an inflated and irrational view of their own value and achievements.

Most importantly, pride is an emotion that requires a character to look at their own selves positively.

Someone who is proud has often developed their own sense of self through reflection and accomplishment. The extent of this in relation to reality determines whether pride will be seen as positive and justified or negative and foolish.

Characters who are proud will often see themselves as worthy of great things and they will be more likely to take risks—this generally makes for an interesting story!

But, if characters exaggerate their accomplishments to cover their lack of self-esteem, they may attack and ridicule others. This becomes an interesting plot and the reader is led to make the intriguing discovery that the character's 'pride' is merely a mask.

The dual role of pride, as both a sin and a virtue makes the emotion a very useful weapon in any writer's arsenal. You could write a story that leads to pride in a positive way or you could write a story where someone's pride has led to their significant downfall—and there are many real life historical events that have shown this!

This chapter will dive into some important types of pride, and explain the different effects that they can have on your audience. By the end, you should be able to write psychologically compelling stories that will keep your reader guessing!

Self-importance

A type of pride is the feeling of self-importance. A character feels important when they realize that their actions are very significant and valuable; they believe that they can change the world, for better or worse. This is often displayed by an increase in confidence, speaking with more authority than they once did, or by acting more ambitiously than they used to.

Allowing their main characters to realize their importance is very important for writers, since it leads to taking bigger risks, and in turn more significant successes and failures.

A character with a strong belief in their own importance will be more likely to put themselves in unfamiliar or uncomfortable situations, to argue and fight for what they believe in, and to do their best to overcome obstacles, even when everybody else thinks that they will fail.

If you've read any story with a hero, it's a pretty safe bet that they realized that they were more important than the average person, and destined for great things. When somebody feels this way, they are probably going to take steps to make their dreams come true, which makes for a great story every time.

Let's take a look at a simple example of importance in fiction: Grant lives in a town with a very old tree in the middle of its main park. Developers have secured permits to knock down the tree so that they can build more houses in its place. One night, Grant has a dream that he is the only one who can stop the tree from being torn down.

Surroundings

681. After the dream, Grant started to spend a lot of time in the park. The squirrels seemed to look at him for an extra second as they passed him on the paths, as if to say, "you're the one who is going to fix this."

682. Even though he was just a kid, Grant felt like the people he passed seemed to nod their head at him and call him "Sir" ever since he started his movement; he had a purpose now, a real adult goal.

683. These days, it was as if Grant walked with a golden crown on his head and the trees bowed down to him, believing that he was their savior.

684. It seemed like wherever he went, conversation turned to the development plans. Grant always spoke up and defended his position; he was an authority on the subject now.

685. New dreams would come to him every couple of nights, visions of huge crowds of people surrounding the old tree, hanging on to his every word.

686. Grant's friends were all surprised at how confident and outspoken he had become, but they were glad that somebody was doing something about the construction project.

687. Grant's newfound interest in activism led to other changes; he used to believe everything that he heard, but now he wondered if there were other motives behind peoples' ideas and opinions.

Appearance

688. Grant closed his eyes and nodded graciously as the famous environmentalist praised his commitment to the cause.

689. Grant raised his chin and looked forward with a self-assured smile, as if he was the subject of a Renaissance portrait.

690. Grant's eyes were bloodshot from lack of sleep, but he didn't care; his actions mattered more than his looks.

691. Grant raised an eyebrow and chuckled when his teacher suggested that he could never save the tree; she'd realize that she had underestimated him soon enough.

692. It was freezing outside the night that it was Grant's turn to guard the tree; his nose started to run and his lips were chapped, but he never stopped smiling, even when he couldn't feel his face anymore.

693. Grant grinned and waggled his eyebrows when the audience began to applaud; people were finally starting to take him seriously.

Actions

694. Between work and school, Grant didn't have a lot of free time, but he'd hand out leaflets about the protest he was planning whenever he had a spare moment; he could sleep when the tree was safe.

695. Grant spent a lot of time researching leadership positions online; if he was going to convince this town to get behind him, he was going to need to do it the right way.

696. Grant paced around his bedroom all night to keep from falling asleep; he had to make sure that his speech was perfect, or else he would let everybody down.

697. Grant chained himself to the old tree; nobody was going to run him over with a bulldozer.

698. Grant stood on a bench and shouted into his megaphone, urging the townspeople to save their beautiful park.

699. Grant used to have trouble paying attention in science class, but now he took lots of notes whenever conservation came up; he knew that he would have to use this information one day.

700. Grant's mother was worried that he would be arrested, but he didn't care; this campaign defined his life, it wasn't going to ruin it.

Ridicule

One thing that almost everybody is afraid of is ridicule. When somebody is ridiculed, the people around them are mocking their beliefs or behavior, acting dismissive and contemptuous of them.

This causes acute embarrassment and is an attack on one's pride, which in turn can make them do more silly things, leading to even more ridicule.

Ridicule is an important emotion for writers to master, because when a character is ridiculed, their reactions are often intense and interesting. Also, since everyone knows what it feels like to be ridiculed, the audience will almost always sympathize with any character that experiences this emotion.

Here is a simple example of a character that has been ridiculed: Stacy had a question about her assignment, but when she tried to get her teacher's attention, instead of saying "Mrs. Parson?" she said, "Mommy?" All of the other students heard her, and burst out laughing. Now they won't stop teasing her about the mistake, and she feels like they'll never let it go.

Surroundings

701. The moment she said it, time seemed to screech to a halt. Stacy knew that she would never live this down.

702. For weeks, conversations seemed to stop whenever Stacy walked into the classroom.

703. One of her classmates, Tom, asked Stacy if her real Mommy knew that her Dad had married the teacher, too.

704. Stacy was invited to her friend's birthday party that weekend, but she faked sick to get out of it. Without teachers to keep them behaved, she knew that the kids would make fun of her all day long.

705. Even though she knew the answer, Stacy wouldn't raise her hand. She was afraid that she would mess up and call Mrs. Parson "Mommy" again, and if she did that her life would be over.

706. Someone had taped a picture of Mrs. Parson to Stacy's locker, and scrawled "I love my Mommy" beneath it.

707. Stacy told her dad that she was too sick to go to school, but he made her get out of bed anyway.

Appearance

708. Stacy gasped, and her face turned deep red.

709. Stacy's eyes went wide with shock, and her jaw dropped.

710. Stacy's bottom lip began to tremble, and tears welled in her eyes.

711. Stacy's eyes darted from side to side, looking for anybody who wasn't laughing at her.

712. Stacy brushed her hair over her face, trying to hide her embarrassment as best as she could.

713. Tears streamed down Stacy's face and her nose began to run.

Actions

714. Stacy peeked around the corner to make sure that nobody was waiting in the hallway to make fun of her.

715. Stacy stood up and ran out of the classroom with her face buried in her hands.

716. Stacy saw some kids her age walking down the sidewalk towards her; she crossed the street to avoid them.

717. Stacy paced around outside the school for fifteen minutes before she could work up the courage to walk inside.

718. Stacy pushed past the bullies and hid in the bathroom.

719. Stacy balled her hands into fists inside of her pockets, furious that Tom was still making fun of her.

720. Stacy held her hands over her mouth, afraid that she was going to throw up and make everything even worse.

Self-righteousness

Another way that a character can show pride is by being self-righteous or judgmental.

A self-righteous character has an overly critical opinion of another character's actions or beliefs. This feeling is somewhat similar to conceit, since it is a negative reaction to other peoples' behavior or lifestyles, but it doesn't come from the same place of superiority.

A self-righteous character may be a little too hard on others for breaking the rules, but they don't necessarily think that they are better than them. Most importantly, judgmental or self-righteous characters' beliefs are usually right; they just express them too strongly.

If utilized correctly, self-righteous characters can be very helpful to include in any story. Since they speak their minds, they can call attention to other character's shortcomings without worrying that their opinions might irritate them. This can highlight the mistakes that your characters have made in your readers' minds, which is very important, especially in complicated situations.

Here is an example of a self-righteous character that can help you to understand how to use this feeling in your own stories: Kris is a vegetarian. He can't help but lecture everyone that he sees eating meat, because he is a very strong believer in animal rights. His opinion is more or less "right"— livestock is often treated inhumanely—but simply eating meat does not make someone a bad person; his tendency to assume this is what makes him judgmental and self-righteous.

Surroundings

721. Kris hated going to the grocery store; seeing all of the people carrying around bundled animal parts like trophies made him sick.

722. Whenever Kris passed a farm, he had to resist the urge to knock on the farmer's door and ask him how he could sleep at night.

723. Kris saw a deer run across the field, and prayed that there weren't any sadistic hunters nearby.

724. Kris' father ate meat with every meal, but he owned two dogs; somehow he didn't see this as hypocritical.

725. Everywhere he looked, Kris saw leather: leather jackets, leather shoes, leather belts. He was surrounded by killers.

726. Even Kris' best friends ate meat in front of him; he felt like he was the only one in the whole town with a sense of morality.

727. Kris started to work at the local pet store, hoping to meet some fellow animal lovers, but the other cashier had the audacity to come to work bundled in a fur coat!

Appearance

728. Kris rolled his eyes and sighed, tired of explaining his lifestyle to people who would never understand it.

729. Kris grimaced as the lunch lady plopped a piece of meatloaf on his plate without asking.

730. Kris clicked his tongue and narrowed his eyes as his friend ordered a veal cutlet.

731. Kris raised an eyebrow and gave his mother a sideways glance as she suggested that he buy a leather belt.

732. Kris bit his lip until it bled, knowing that he'd be fired if he made one more comment about his boss' lunch order.

733. Kris winced, then glared at his father as he suggested that pigs couldn't feel pain.

Actions

734. Kris leaned against the fence with folded arms, shaking his head as he watched his best friend cook a steak in the backyard.

735. When his mother told him that there was meat in the chili, he spat it into a napkin.

736. Kris' uncle suggested that they go to the horse races that afternoon; Kris just turned around and left the room.

737. When the man told Kris that he was a hunter, he just raised his arms in exasperation and looked to the sky for support.

738. Kris' father gave him a leather wallet for his birthday as a joke; he tossed it into the trash can right in front of him.

739. Kris asked the woman how she could claim to be a good person with a mouthful of chicken.

740. Kris wanted to open up the gates and free the cows, but he contented himself with giving the farmer a dirty look and deliberately spitting on his driveway.

CHAPTER NINE

Sadness

One of the most universal and difficult of all emotions is sadness. Sadness is the opposite of happiness: it is characterized by sorrow, misery, depression, and grief.

People become sad because their plans are failing, because terrible and tragic things are happening to them or to people that they care about, or just because they're having a bad day.

There are lots of different types of sadness, and they have lots of different intensities and symptoms. Each one of them can create its own unique reaction in your readers.

Any writer will tell you that learning how to illustrate sadness is a very important part of the craft. Most great stories don't have happy endings. They focus on the struggles and hardships of life, and their main characters don't live happily ever after.

By slowly increasing the sadness that your characters feel—or by suddenly plunging them deep into despair—they will start to feel like their goals are hopeless, and really focus on the difficulty of their situations.

This will make your audience connect with your characters on an emotional level; if they've been in a similar situation, reading about another version of it may help them process and understand their own feelings. Evoking such a strong response from your readers is the most powerful and rewarding part of storytelling.

Like happiness, sadness is a basic and universal idea, which makes it challenging to describe effectively. This chapter is full of specific examples of different types of sadness, which will produce very different effects on your audience. By deciding which type of sadness is best for your character, and using descriptions that are best suited to it, you'll be sure to turn your page-turner into a tear-jerker!

Abandonment

One of the most important versions of sadness is abandonment. A character feels abandoned when they have been deserted, betrayed, or cast off, especially by someone that they care about.

Characters experiencing abandonment might lash out at those closest to them, have difficulty trusting others, or collapse into despair. This emotion affects every aspect of a character's life, and will quickly consume them if they can't escape it.

Writers often use abandonment as one of a character's main personality traits. Characters that feel abandoned will be slow to trust protagonists, but they can be won over eventually through consistent displays of solidarity and kindness. If someone says or does something that reminds the abandoned character of their original betrayer, they may snap and act in an abnormally aggressive or intense manner.

These aspects of their personalities make abandoned characters natural conflict-generators; they almost never make situations easier, and they usually make them much worse. More conflict means more drama and more reader attention!

Here is a simple example of a character with abandonment issues: Carol's mother disappeared when she was young, leaving her and her father to fend for themselves. Because of this, Carol has difficulty trusting people, especially older women and authority figures.

Surroundings

741. Without her mother there, the house felt so empty and strange. Each room seemed eerily quiet, as if they were keeping secrets.

742. The laughter that used to ring throughout the house was now replaced with absolute silence—the kind of silence that made you want to shift on your seat uncomfortably.

743. Carol used to wish on shooting stars but now, they were meaningless; she'd made it this far in life without a mother.

744. The piano, once pristine, was now covered in cobwebs and its wooden panels, eaten by mould—a reminder of the time passed since Carol had waited for her mother.

745. The phone never rang but today, it did, and she was suspicious. What if it were her mother wishing to come back to make her feel even worse?

746. Each room in the house seemed darker—the light that used to pour in seemed to disappear and the plants drooped miserably.

747. Instead of sitting at home alone, Carol began taking long, aimless walks after school but that didn't help—whenever she saw a mother and child tenderly holding hands, the sky around her darkened.

Appearance

748. Carol's bottom lip would start to quiver whenever she thought about the day her mother left.

749. Carol sighed and looked out the window forlornly, half-expecting to see her mother walking down the driveway.

750. After years of obsessing over her mother's departure, Carol's face was creased with deep worry-lines.

751. Carol closed her eyes and groaned, wishing that she could just forget about her mother entirely.

752. When her father told her that her mother had left for good, Carol's jaw dropped and her eyelids began to twitch.

753. Carol twisted her mouth and squinted, trying to decide if the woman ahead of her in line was her mother.

Actions

754. Carol sat on her front porch until after dark and waited for her mother to come home. Eventually, she fell asleep; her Dad picked her up and carried her to bed.

755. Carol wrote her mother countless letters asking her why she'd decided to leave, but she never mailed them.

756. Carol began to wear her mother's brand of perfume, because it reminded her of the time that they'd spent together.

757. Carol often wondered why her mother didn't love her enough to remain in her life.

758. Whenever her Dad was late coming home from work, Carol would send him lots of frantic text messages, determined to learn what was holding him up.

759. Carol started studying extra hard for her exams; maybe if she got straight A's, her mother would return.

760. Carol tried to stay cheerful in front of her Dad, but she would often stay up late into the night, crying and wishing that her mother was there.

Depression

One of the most severe and powerful forms of sadness is depression. A depressed character is overcome by dejection and despondency.

The things that they once loved to do no longer give them any pleasure, and almost every aspect of their life starts to feel like a burden to them. If left unchecked, a depressed character may begin to question the value of life itself.

Depression is one of the most challenging and terrible types of emotion that a person can experience, which makes it a good candidate for storytelling. One of the major purposes of literature is to explore complex and difficult emotions, so it's natural that depression is a major theme in lots of stories.

Depressed characters don't see the beauty of everything around them, and they don't place much value in their own happiness. Often, someone close to the main character will become depressed, and the main character's mission will be to alleviate that person's depression.

If you can illustrate this feeling effectively, your stories will help your audience to feel better about themselves and overcome difficult periods in their own lives. This is one of the most valuable gifts that a writer can give his or her reader.

Here is a basic example of depression that you can use in your own work: Stephanie's husband of four years, Derek, has recently left her and the family. Since Derek was such an important part of her life for so long, Stephanie slips into a deep depression, unable to see how she will ever come to terms with the breakup, or find happiness again.

Surroundings

761. Since Derek left, the whole world looked washed out and gray to Stephanie.

762. Stephanie and Derek had a lot of the same favorite bands—it was one of the reasons why they became friends in the first place. Now Stephanie couldn't listen to half of the songs in her library without tearing up.

763. Stephanie's phone rang, but she didn't pick it up. If it was anyone other than Derek, she didn't want to talk to them. Come to think of it, she didn't really want to talk to him, either.

764. Stephanie's mind was constantly buzzing and numb. She couldn't pay attention in school, she kept getting lectured about her productivity at work—everything was falling apart.

765. At the party, Stephanie couldn't see anything else other than blurs of darkness. The music? It was now just long heavy thumps and pauses.

766. The sky seemed to be tinged with a permanent blue and the sun, devoid of light and dull.

767. The walls seemed to cave her in and Stephanie knew this wasn't the end of the world, but it certainly felt that way to her.

Appearance

768. Stephanie tried to smile for her mother's benefit, but it came out like a twisted grimace.

769. Stephanie's eyes were glazed over; they barely flickered as people passed in and out of her field of vision.

770. Stephanie's eyes were red and puffy from spending the whole night crying.

771. Stephanie couldn't even work up the energy to frown.

772. Stephanie bit her lip and squinted, trying to keep from bursting into tears again.

773. Stephanie frowned and gazed hopelessly at the last photograph she and Derek had taken together.

Actions

774. Stephanie stopped showering regularly and picking out cute outfits. What was the point if Derek wasn't there to compliment her?

775. Stephanie didn't bother to do her makeup or fix her hair; between that and her disinterested gaze, people kept asking her if she was sick.

776. Stephanie snatched up every item in her room that reminded her of Derek in a fit of rage, but when it came time to throw the box away, she just sank back onto her bed and covered her face with her pillow.

777. Stephanie stopped going to work altogether. Her boss called her to fire her after she missed four shifts in a row, but she just shrugged carelessly.

778. Stephanie shuffled around her apartment with her head drooped down, dragging her feet on the tile floor.

779. Stephanie's friend told her to make a list of all the things that she was grateful for; after an hour of sitting in front of a blank page, she gave up and went back to bed.

780. Stephanie slept until three in the afternoon, then drove over to the grocery store in her pajamas and flip flops; she didn't have the motivation to take a shower.

Despair

Another severe form of sadness is despair. A character feels despair when they have lost all sense of hope. They no longer believe that anything good can come of their situation.

Characters experiencing despair may become withdrawn, hysterical, or nihilistic, since they don't see the point of trying to move past the tragedy that has befallen them.

Despair is a wonderful emotion for writers to take advantage of, because it illustrates a massive change in the character that experiences it. Perhaps they have spent the bulk of their story brimming with hope and optimism, or faith that their struggles would be worth it in the end.

Now that a final, soul-crushing blow has been struck, they no longer know how to move forward. This significant change of heart will cause readers to become very sympathetic towards their situation, and hope that they will find a way to overcome their despair. If they do, readers will be ecstatic; if they don't, readers will be devastated.

Either reaction is very powerful, and would help to make any story resonate with its audience.

Here is a basic example of despair that you can use as a template for your own work: A few years ago, Adam was diagnosed with cancer. He followed his doctors' orders to the letter, and the disease seemed to be in remission. Now, just when he thought he'd beaten it altogether, his doctor has informed him that the cancer is back, and worse than ever. Adam still has a chance to survive if he continues to fight and undergo treatment, but he doesn't think he has enough energy to go through the whole ordeal again.

Surroundings

781. After he hung up the phone, Adam looked out his window. The sun was shining, but he could see dark clouds on the horizon.

782. Adam's family were very supportive of him, pledging to help him beat this thing once and for all, but he wasn't sure that he could bring himself to start from square one.

783. It was spring, and the flowers were finally in bloom. Adam used to love this time of year, but somehow it didn't make him feel any better.

784. Adam felt like every doctor who talked to him secretly knew that his time was up; he could see it in the somber faces that they made when they thought he wasn't looking.

785. Adam knew that he was bringing everybody down; sometimes he wished that he could just get it over with and die already.

786. Adam watched the young father effortlessly hoist his daughter onto his back. He nearly started to cry; he hadn't had the strength to do that in months.

787. The days flew by without Adam noticing; he spent most of his time curled up in bed, trying not to think about his own mortality.

Appearance

788. Adam's eyes were dull and distant; it was like he wasn't even there.

789. Adam's face was gaunt and expressionless; if somebody came up and hit him, he probably wouldn't have even noticed.

790. Tears streamed down Adam's cheeks as he shook his head from side to side; he had no hope left.

791. Adam looked up into the sky with an open mouth and pleading eyes, begging God to have mercy on him.

792. Adam had been staring down at the table with widened eyes and raised eyebrows for what felt like hours; he couldn't remember the last time he blinked.

793. Adam's lips were chapped and dry, and his face was contorted into a mask of pain.

Actions

794. Adam stopped shaving the day that he was diagnosed. Why bother, he thought, the radiation will make it all fall out anyway.

795. Adam started skipping his chemo appointments; what was the point? He was going to die anyway, why should he postpone the inevitable?

796. Adam fell to his knees in the middle of the supermarket, sobbing so hard that his whole body shook.

797. Adam had always taken care of himself, but now he ate fast food for every meal. A few extra calories here and there weren't going to make him feel any worse.

798. The doorbell kept ringing, but Adam just stuffed his head underneath his pillow to block out the sound. He couldn't bring himself to have another conversation about how he was holding up.

799. Adam went around his house shutting all the blinds, then sat in the living room with the lights off. He wanted to be surrounded by darkness.

800. After Adam pulled into the driveway, he sat in his car and screamed at the top of his lungs; it made him feel a little better.

Disillusionment

Another interesting form of sadness is disillusionment. A character feels disillusioned when someone who they previously respected or trusted does something to violate their respect or trust.

This is similar to betrayal, in that it represents a rapid negative change in one character's opinion towards another, but disillusionment is unique in that it usually doesn't come as a response to a personal slight. In other words, a character doesn't become disillusioned because another character does something to harm them, they become disillusioned because the other character behaves in a way that makes them lose respect for them indirectly.

Disillusionment can be a powerful tool in any writer's toolbox, because it involves a major change of opinion on the part of one character.

Often, the character causing the disillusionment is a mentor or role model for the protagonist—someone that the audience has found likable and sympathetic throughout the story—who, once the curtain is lifted, turns out to be less pure and righteous than they originally appeared.

This change, if illustrated effectively, will cause the audience to go from loving a character to absolutely hating them in the course of a few paragraphs!

Great stories usually involve emotionally-complex situations, and properly harnessing the power of disillusionment is definitely a good way to reach that goal.

Let's take a look at a basic example of disillusionment: Kristen has always wanted to be a pop star, and she has been obsessed with Tatiana for years. When she finally gets backstage tickets to one of her concerts, Kristen is overjoyed—until she discovers that Tatiana is self-centered and mean.

Surroundings

801. Only moments ago, Tatiana looked like a goddess gliding around backstage; now all Kristen could see was a grotesque troll with bloodshot eyes.

802. Kristen had dreamed about meeting Tatiana in person for months, but now, her once lyrical voice was distorted into the gnarls of a doberman.

803. The excitement and energy in the room evaporated in a second and the grand balloons deflated. Tatiana didn't deserve any kind of adoration or praise.

804. The gleaming poster of Tatiana was a fake; just like fool's gold—Kristen scratched the surface and saw what was really there—a little brat.

805. On the outside, Tatiana's face was perfect, but once she opened her mouth, it was as if a blazing fire was released.

806. The once brilliant dance moves that Tatiana performed were now dull and animatronic to Kristen.

807. Kristen felt so stupid for obsessing over a musician who couldn't make it through a five minute conversation without even looking away from the mirror for just one second; she would never make that mistake again.

Appearance

808. Kristen blinked slowly then widened her eyes, shocked that the drama queen standing in front of her had written all of those beautiful songs.

809. Kristen raised an eyebrow and stared at the gushing fans; why weren't they feeling just as disappointed as she was?

810. Kristen felt like crying, but she focused on channeling her disappointment into hostility, narrowing her eyes and gritting her teeth.

811. Instead of following Tatiana's every move, Kristen stared off into the distance, looking at nothing in particular with a dull stare.

812. Kristen's jaw dropped and she shook her head slowly as she watched Tatiana's rabid fans make fools of themselves. She couldn't believe that she was just like them only a few hours ago.

813. After five minutes of listening to Tatiana whine and complain, Kristen's eyes were glazed over and her mouth felt dry; the girl standing in front of her wasn't her hero anymore.

Actions

814. The second she got home, Kristen threw all of her copies of Tatiana's CDs into the trash. Her mental image of Tatiana was now turned upside down and spoiled.

815. Kristen had brought a poster along with her, hoping that Tatiana would sign it, but now she didn't even bother asking for an autograph.

816. Kristen folded her arms tightly across her chest and leaned petulantly against a wall, determined to show Tatiana that she was unimpressed by her behavior.

817. Kristen shifted her weight from one foot to the other as Tatiana screamed at her makeup artist; not only was it sad to see her former idol throwing such a big tantrum, it was embarrassing.

818. Kristen sunk down to the floor and buried her face in her hands. She'd modeled her entire personality on Tatiana's; if *she* was a whiny jerk, what did that make her?

819. For years, Kristen had fantasized about getting Tatiana's lyrics tattooed on her arm. Now she rubbed at the spot she'd picked out absentmindedly, as if the very idea had made it unclean.

820. Kristen used to doodle phrases from Tatiana's songs in the margins of her notebook. After the show, she tore out every single page that she'd ruined with the horrible pop star's lyrics.

Embarrassment

Embarrassment is a type of sadness that manifests itself through self-consciousness, awkwardness, or shame.

A character feels embarrassed when his or her foolish actions are perceived by others, or even when they just think that others have witnessed them. They may wish that they could run away from the situation, or lash out aggressively in an attempt to conceal their embarrassment.

Embarrassment can be used to achieve a variety of effects; embarrassing situations are the backbone of literary comedy, but they can also make a sad story even sadder. By making the audience recall situations when they felt embarrassed, the writer can generate a lot of sympathy for their characters very quickly.

Here are some examples of different ways that you can show embarrassment in your own stories.

Surroundings

821. When she walked into the room, it seemed like everyone stopped talking and stared. They knew.

822. Even though they tried their best to swallow their giggles, it was as through their muffled sounds were rings of hysterical laughter that were broadcast over loudspeaker.

823. She wanted to dig a hole in her backyard and crawl into it.

824. All of his neighbors must have been peeking at him through their blinds, laughing or shaking their heads.

825. She knew that the security camera had recorded the whole thing. Before long, it would be posted online and start spreading around the world. This was exactly the sort of thing that went viral.

826. The walls started to spin—all he could now see were fingers pointing at him and millions of huge mouths opening up, ready to swallow him whole.

827. The kids on the swing set were just dangling there with their mouthes wide open. She wanted to scream at them, "mind your own business!"

Appearance

828. He was the perfect picture of calmness, but inside, he was stomping his feet and tearing out his hair.

829. She looked like if she stopped smiling for a second, she would burst into tears.

830. His bottom lip started to quiver, and his face flushed until he was beet red.

831. She would have blushed, but she didn't have the energy.

832. She winced, knowing that she would never live this down.

833. She felt hot tears sting the corners of her eyes, but she wouldn't let them have the satisfaction of seeing them.

Actions

834. He turned and ran for the bathroom, although he clearly had no reason to go there now.

835. She collapsed onto the floor and buried her head in her hands, too tired to even bother to hide her reaction.

836. He swallowed hard, then tried to keep his voice from shaking.

837. She pinched her arm, hoping that the pain would distract her, but it didn't work.

838. He gazed at his shoes like a twelve year old that just got in trouble.

839. He absently scratched at the back of his neck, as if he could remove whatever made him act like such an idiot from his brain stem.

840. He started picking at the scab on the back of his hand that never healed, never went away.

Guilt

One of the most complex and interesting forms of sadness is guilt. A character feels guilty when they feel responsible for doing something wrong, especially if someone else has been blamed for their wrongdoing.

Guilty characters will usually feel worse and worse as time goes on, until they can't live with their secrets any longer and they force themselves to accept the consequences of their actions. In the mean time, they often find ways to punish themselves or make an already bad situation worse in their attempts to overcome the guilt.

Since it is a complicated emotion that becomes more severe over time, guilt is a great emotion to use as the centerpiece of a story.

The character in question often starts in a place of happiness—or at least neutrality—and acts in a selfish or thoughtless manner for almost no reason.

Then, the guilt starts to set in.

Their behavior becomes more and more erratic and their thoughts become more and more self-hating, until they either lose the opportunity to make up for their actions or come clean and accept the consequences that they have coming to them.

The uncertainty about which path they will ultimately choose is inherently interesting, and will keep your audience reading until they find out what decision the character makes.

Let's look at a simple situation that illustrates guilt, which you can use in your own stories: When Brenda is fooling around at home, she accidentally knocks over her mother's favorite vase, and it breaks into a thousand pieces. Her mother automatically blames Brenda's sister, Tiff, because she is usually the trouble-maker. Tiff swears that she didn't do it, but no one believes her. Brenda has gotten away unpunished, but she slowly finds herself overcome with guilt.

Surroundings

841. The mirror on her bedroom wall no longer appeared to reflect her but also, her lie; she couldn't even stand to look at herself after what she'd done.

842. It was as if Brenda were freely standing outside a cage that now enclosed her little sister—a cage that Brenda put her in.

843. Her little sister's cries could be heard through the wall; Brenda hung her head in shame and stared forlornly at the ground.

844. Brenda was sure that the universe was going to punish her for her deceit; sooner or later, she was going to get what she deserved.

845. Brenda kept convincing herself that she was about to go downstairs and confess, but she couldn't force her hand to turn the doorknob.

846. There was a TV in her room, but Brenda refused to turn it on; denying herself this little pleasure made her feel a bit less despicable.

847. Sitting at the dinner table with her family, Brenda felt like she was going to stand up and tell the truth at any moment; all the lies were eating her up inside.

Appearance

848. Brenda scrunched up her eyes and winced when Tiff got grounded for a week, all because of her.

849. The second that the lie escaped from Brenda's lips, her whole body went cold. All of the color drained from her face, and she let her mouth hang wide open, like she'd just seen a ghost.

850. Whenever she closed her eyes, Brenda couldn't help but picture her Mom lecturing her about how honesty was the most important virtue.

851. Brenda's eyes widened when she realized that she was going to get away with it, but the frown never left her face.

852. Whenever her parents mentioned the incident, Brenda pursed her lips and nervously shifted her eyes from left to right.

853. Brenda gritted her teeth and cringed; how could she keep letting Tiff take the blame?

Actions

854. Brenda wrung her hands and shifted back and forth on the balls of her feet the entire time that her Dad was talking to her.

855. Brenda picked out some of her favorite outfits and gave them to Tiff; maybe doing something kind for her sister would make her feel better.

856. When her Mom mentioned the vase, Brenda made a lame excuse and scurried out of the room.

857. Brenda hid in her room all night, trying not to think about how she'd stabbed Tiff in the back.

858. On her way to the bathroom, Brenda tiptoed past Tiff's room as sneakily as possible. She knew that if she talked to her sister, she would end up confessing the whole thing.

859. Brenda started shoving clothes into her backpack, planning to run away from home, but she stopped when she realized that she'd still be beating herself up no matter where she went.

860. Brenda wrote a note to Tiff, admitting that she was the one who broke the vase, but she lost her nerve and tore it into tiny pieces.

Loneliness

Another form of sadness that is often found in literature is loneliness. A character feels lonely when they are disconnected from others, either physically or emotionally.

Sometimes, lonely characters will feel withdrawn from the people around them. Other times, they may desperately cling to any scraps of social interaction that they find, which usually results in awkward conversations and further isolation.

Loneliness can be a very valuable character trait in many stories. Lonely characters are often very introspective, which leads to interesting narration.

Additionally, all lonely characters have a goal: to become less lonely!

This built in motivation helps writers, because it gives the characters something to strive towards, which makes them more multi-dimensional and interesting.

Here is an example of a lonely character that you can branch off from in your own writing: Mitch decided to go on a month-long backpacking trip by himself. He thought that he would have fun and get to know himself better, but after a few days without talking to or even seeing another person, he was overcome with loneliness.

Surroundings

861. The view from the trail was breathtaking, but all Mitch could think about was how he was probably the only human for miles in any direction.

862. Lying on his back in the field, Mitch watched planes pass by far overhead, wishing that he was on one of them.

863. He was expecting that the valley would contain all kinds of creatures, but when he arrived, it was a sparse wasteland of cracked clay with just one single stem of dried grass.

864. A week into the journey, Mitch really started to lose it. He spent fifteen minutes arguing with a squirrel who dropped an acorn on his head before he realized how ridiculous he must have looked.

865. Mitch felt like the world had ended, and he was the only one who'd survived.

866. Mitch carved messages into some trees, hoping that another solitary camper would come across them one day and feel less alone than he did right now.

867. Mitch scratched a smiley face into a boulder and spent the night lounging by the fire, chatting with it. He knew he was acting crazy, but it made him feel a little better.

Appearance

868. Mitch soon adopted an expression of pure neutrality; there was nobody around for him to smile for.

869. Mitch looked down at the cluster of houses in the valley with eyes full of longing and grief.

870. Mitch's lips were cracked and dry after a week of complete silence.

871. Mitch closed his eyes and pictured his friends having fun far away from him, but his frown only deepened even further.

872. Mitch thought he saw someone approaching him on the path; he let a hopeful grin creep across his face, but when he squinted he saw that it was only a deer.

873. His eyes were red from crying, but he didn't feel self-conscious; nobody was here to witness his fragility.

Actions

874. Mitch fell to his knees and sighed. He wanted to scream at the top of his lungs, but nobody was close enough to hear him.

875. Every night, Mitch dreamed of his family and friends back home, and every morning, he woke up alone.

876. Mitch kept checking his phone every few hours, hoping that he could spend a few minutes talking with someone—anyone—but he never had any service.

877. Mitch wrote letters to all of his friends; he would probably never send them, but it cheered him up a little.

878. Mitch started hiking twice as fast as usual, hoping to overtake another group of campers, or at least to finish this terrible trip a few days early.

879. Mitch had gone so long without saying his own name that it took him a few minutes to remember what it was.

880. Mitch scaled a cliff face high up on the mountain, hoping to spot somebody nearby. He sat on top of it for hours, but nobody came.

Pity

The last type of sadness that we'll focus on is pity. A character feels pity when the suffering of others causes them sorrow. When a character feels pity for someone, they will often go out of their way to help that person, hoping that they can make them feel a little better.

Characters most often feel pity for those that are close to them, but a complete stranger could also evoke the emotion in them, especially if they have experienced a similar misfortune in the past.

Pity can be a versatile and useful tool for fiction writers. The emotion usually manifests itself through the actions of a character—i.e., they help the object of their pity somehow—so it can be used to advance the plot in a very natural and believable way.

Often, when it seems like everything is stacked up against a protagonist and there is no way for them to reach their goal, another character will come along and take pity on them, which breaks them out of their rut and sets them back on track for victory.

Here is an example of pity that you can apply to your own stories: Bella notices a homeless child has started begging in front of the building where she works. Since she was once homeless, Bella takes pity on the child, and decides to help her improve her life.

Surroundings

881. Although it was a warm, sunny day, Bella felt a chill run through her when she saw the girl picking through the garbage, looking for food.

882. Bella couldn't sleep—she was rugged up in layers of soft cashmere while she knew that the girl was out there somewhere, being pelted with heavy freezing rain.

883. On her lunch break outside, Bella couldn't concentrate on her book; she kept glancing over the cover at the little girl wandering around the sidewalk and rattling her tin.

884. Whenever Bella walked past the little girl, she would hear the sounds of rattling tin and adults scoffing. It sent her back in time to the year that she was homeless.

885. Bella couldn't focus at work; why should she be paid for tapping on her keyboard in an air-conditioned room, while that girl was scrambling around the concrete trying to find just one coin?

886. Bella's home was like a warm bear hug—safe and cosy, it was another world compared to the little girl who had to run away from stray dogs and use her gangly arm as a shield against the weather.

887. Every piece of furniture in Bella's apartment reminded her of what the little girl lacked—her cushy bed now reminded her of the tattered cardboard that the little girl was forced to sleep on.

Appearance

888. Bella stared at the girl with knitted brows and eyes tinged with worry.

889. Bella grinned at the little girl, even as she felt the tears welling in her eyes.

890. Bella frowned deeply and bit her lip, frustrated by her helplessness.

891. Bella winced when she saw the girl clutch her empty belly.

892. Bella closed her eyes, trying to imagine a world where such injustices didn't exist, but it didn't make her feel any better.

893. Bella pursed her lips and squinted, wishing that she could do something to help.

Actions

894. Bella fished a few dollars out of her wallet and gave them to the girl. She didn't have much money to spare, but she knew that the girl needed it much more than she did.

895. Bella knew that there was nothing she could do to really improve a complete stranger's life, but that didn't stop her from spending all her free time trying to think of a plan.

896. When Bella was making herself lunch, she thought about the hungry little girl and packed an extra sandwich, just in case she ran into her.

897. Every time Bella had seen the little girl, she'd been wearing the same tattered old sweater. She rummaged through her drawers and filled a bag with some outfits she hadn't worn in years, hoping that the little girl might like them.

898. Bella knew from experience that a little bit of human kindness went a long way; she picked out a huge lollipop at the corner store, hoping that it might help the little girl to forget about her situation for a little while.

899. Bella gasped and clapped her hand over her mouth when she saw the little girl burst into tears.

900. Bella couldn't concentrate on work when she knew the little girl was outside in the cold. She clocked out a few minutes early and offered to buy her a cup of tea.

Withdrawal

One type of sadness that any character can feel is withdrawal. A character feels withdrawn when he or she no longer wants to communicate with the outside world, or participate in it. This can occur when something very sad happens to the character, or when they no longer enjoy doing something that once made them happy.

It can be useful to have a character become withdrawn in your stories, because it will show the readers that they are going through emotional changes. The contrast between their actions before and after feeling withdrawn will increase reader interest, and further illustrate the difficulties that they are experiencing.

There are a lot of different situations that can cause a character to feel withdrawn.

Below, we'll use a simple one to show you how to capture this emotion in your stories. Frank's best friend, Steve, has recently moved far away from their hometown. Since Frank misses Steve, he starts to feel withdrawn, no longer taking pleasure in his day to day life.

Surroundings

901. The flowers were just starting to bloom, but Frank walked past them without noticing.

902. Frank could hear birds chirping outside of his window; he shut it and closed the curtains.

903. It had been a while since Frank stepped foot outside the house. In that time, every crack and bump in the wall was familiar to him and his eyes were so used to the glow of artificial light that they had difficulty adjusting to sunlight.

904. A bunch of the other kids were outside laughing and playing in the yard, but Frank couldn't bring himself to walk over and talk to them.

905. Frank knew that he should be happy that summer break had started, but he just stayed inside, watching tv.

906. Frank's mother wanted to take him to the beach to cheer him up; he went along, but didn't set foot in the ocean.

907. The sun was shining, but everything looked hazy and dull.

Appearance

908. Frank blinked and let his eyes glaze over.

909. Frank pursed his lips and rubbed his temples.

910. Frank frowned and knitted his brow.

911. Frank gave a little half-smile, but he didn't mean it.

912. Frank was staring off into the distance, looking like he was thinking about something a thousand miles away.

913. Frank raised an eyebrow and scratched his chin, unimpressed by the gift.

Actions

914. Even though he missed him so badly, Frank let Steve's call go unanswered.

915. His favorite show came on, but Frank just yawned and shut off the tv.

916. Frank knew that his mother was trying to cheer him up, but he didn't have the energy to pretend to care.

917. Frank's new neighbor came over to introduce himself, but Frank just hid in his room.

918. Nothing could make Frank laugh anymore, not even his favorite joke book.

919. One of Frank's classmates waved at him, but he walked past without saying hello.

920. Frank knew that Steve would want him to have fun at the party, but he just sulked in the corner with his arms folded.

CHAPTER TEN

Surprise

Surprise is a response to the unexpected; it takes many forms, both positive and negative, but its expression is almost always involuntary and intense.

Characters become surprised when situations that they are involved in take unpredictable twists and turns. Depending on the nature of the events at hand, this emotion can manifest itself in lots of different ways, all of which can be used to create valuable and entertaining stories.

Mastering surprise is an essential step in becoming a great fiction writer, because this emotion serves a distinct purpose: advancing the plot in a unique and interesting way. If nothing happens in your story to surprise any of your characters, then chances are that it won't surprise your readers, either.

Predictable stories are boring, and the last thing that you want to do is to write a boring story. By coming up with unexpected twists that surprise your characters—and even yourself—you'll make sure that your work stays fresh and interesting, which will entertain your audience and keep them turning the pages.

However, once you come up with a great plot twist, your job is only halfway over; you need to decide how your characters will react to the unexpected by choosing the most appropriate form of surprise and making sure that it comes across to your readers.

This chapter will dive into several of the most important types of surprise, and explain the different effects that they can have on your audience. By the end, you should be able to keep your readers on the edges of their seats in no time!

Astonishment

One of the most basic forms of surprise is astonishment. A character feels astonished when they are very impressed or amazed, usually by the actions of another character.

Since this is an inherently positive version of surprise, it is often used for comedic effect. Astonished characters will usually express their disbelief that someone who they thought they knew very well could perform an action that they didn't think was possible.

Astonishment is a good emotion for fiction writers to use because it helps make otherwise unbelievable turns of events seem real. If something wild and crazy happens in your story, but none of the characters react as if it is out of the ordinary, chances are that your audience isn't going to buy it.

However, if one of your characters expresses their disbelief in the form of astonishment, it will make the situation feel more realistic and plausible, which will buy you a lot of credit from your audience.

Here is a simple example of astonishment that you can use in your own work: Clarence is a mediocre basketball player, but at the end of the most important game of the season, he somehow ends up with the ball when the score is tied. At the last second, he lobs it across the court towards the net, and makes a basket against all odds, winning the game.

Surroundings

921. The moment the ball left his hand, Clarence knew that it was going to go in, but he held his breath, as if the slightest puff of air could send it off course.

922. Clarence felt time slow to a crawl, already knowing that he would remember this moment for the rest of his life.

923. The ball glided through the hoop a hundred feet away, just as the buzzer sounded. Clarence's jaw dropped; he just couldn't believe that he'd made the game-winning basket.

924. The television screen overhead kept replaying the moment over and over as the crowd stood on their tiptoes and oohed and aahed at the lucky shot.

925. The ground shook as the crowd started to jump and clasp their hands on their cheeks in sheer disbelief.

926. The crowd stood there—their faces slack but eyes wide and glued to the leaderboard. After a burst of five short and harsh gasps, huge cheers erupted in the stalls.

927. The crowd rushed the court and hoisted Clarence onto their shoulders. He was still in a daze; he couldn't believe that this was happening to him.

Appearance

928. Clarence felt like his jaw might hit the floor if he wasn't careful.

929. Clarence blinked hard, making sure that this wasn't a trick of the light.

930. Once he was sure that the basket was good, a slow smile crept across his face, rapidly turning into an ear-to-ear grin.

931. As the ball hovered closer and closer to the basket, Clarence bit his lip and winced, praying that nothing would go wrong.

932. With shock-widened eyes, Clarence looked down at his hands; how could they have pulled this off?

933. Clarence raised his eyebrows so far up into his forehead his eyes began to water.

Actions

934. Clarence pinched himself in the arm to make sure that he wasn't dreaming; he wasn't.

935. Clarence sank to his knees, as chaos exploded all around him.

936. Clarence was pulled to the sidelines and asked to give an interview, but he just shook his head and wandered off towards the locker room; he needed time to process this.

937. Clarence was so focused on the shot that he felt like he blacked out for a few seconds; when he snapped out of it, he found himself with his hands raised over his head, pumping his fists in the air in celebration.

938. When he walked past a mirror in the locker room, Clarence realized that his mouth was still hanging wide open, and snapped it shut; he must have looked like a crazy person out there!

939. Clarence rubbed his eyes and glanced over at the scoreboard, certain that the ball couldn't have gone in; it must have been a trick of the light.

940. Clarence shook his head in disbelief, then started to laugh in spite of himself; it was so strange to be the center of attention for once.

Confusion

A subtler form of surprise is confusion. When a character feels confused, they are extremely puzzled about the situation that they've found themselves in.

Confused characters often become distracted and derailed, refocusing all of their energy towards processing the surprise that they are experiencing.

Confusion can be useful for writers in several different ways. Like the other types of surprise, it is natural for people to become perplexed when placed in strange situations, so including this emotion helps to make both your characters and your plots feel more realistic and believable.

Additionally, confused characters tend to dwell on the situation that they are in while they try to make sense of it, which can assist you in slowing down the pacing of your stories at especially powerful or interesting moments, in order to make sure that they create as much impact as possible.

Capitalizing on these aspects of confusion will go a long way towards making a good story great.

Below, you'll find a basic example of confusion that you can use as a template: Liz was sure that her friend Dylan would support her decision to quit her job, but he chastised her for being spoiled and foolish instead. She becomes confused, and tries to figure out why her friend disagrees with her so strongly.

Surroundings

941. Even though Liz's room was spotless, it seemed as though her bed was upside down and that her closet had been turned upside down.

942. It was as if question marks seemed to float through every memory Liz had of their friendship—what else was she wrong about?

943. Suddenly, it felt like as if day were night and night were day—Liz's world had been turned upside down; why would Dylan disagree with her?

944. Liz started to question everything—when she reached out for her toothbrush, she wasn't sure whether she usually used her left or right hand.

945. After she finished her report, Liz knocked on her manager's door only to realize she had knocked on the janitor's closet. If she could make such a simple mistake, perhaps she was wrong about her decision?

946. Liz started to feel unsettled. There's was something wrong in her office —but she couldn't quite tell what it was. She felt as though she had entered a house with the gas stove left on; the atmosphere was dense and strange, thought apparently invisible to her eyes.

947. Every side of her cubicle office seemed to be looming over her and she felt cornered and trapped. The cubicle opening was always on her right side, but now it was on her left.

Appearance

948. Liz was totally bewildered; she arched an eyebrow and pursed her lips tightly.

949. Liz furrowed her brow and squinted at the message from Dylan; he must have misunderstood her somehow.

950. Liz let her jaw go slack as her eyes widened; she didn't see this coming at all.

951. Liz's hair was wild and unkempt from hours of scratching her head and rubbing her temples. She'd driven herself half crazy thinking about it, but she still couldn't figure out why Dylan would disagree with her.

952. Completely taken aback, Liz just stood there blinking slowly as her eyes wavered back and forth.

953. Liz closed her eyes and gnawed on her lower lip, trying to think of another way to approach Dylan's response to her message, but nothing she could think of made any sense.

Actions

954. Liz tried to make a list of reasons why Dylan might disagree with her, but she couldn't come up with a single one.

955. Liz decided to go on a long walk, hoping that the exercise would make Dylan's reasoning a little bit clearer to her. When she returned home two hours later, covered in sweat, she still hadn't come up with any plausible explanation.

956. Liz paced back and forth in her bedroom, having a mental argument with Dylan, but she couldn't even figure out what his half of the conversation would sound like.

957. Liz dove onto her bed and screamed into her pillow; if she couldn't figure out a solution to this crisis soon, she was going to drive herself crazy.

958. Liz stayed up late into the night, lying in her bed and wondering what Dylan's problem was.

959. Liz read Dylan's message over and over, scratching her head absentmindedly. She couldn't make any sense of it.

960. Liz started chewing her nails frantically, a nervous habit that popped up whenever she was caught completely off-guard.

Shock

The final version of surprise that we'll look at is also one of the most intense: shock.

When a character is shocked, they are so overcome with surprise that they freeze up; briefly, they can no longer function as they once did. The situation that they find themselves in is so negative and unpredictable that it requires all of their mental power to process it.

Shock can be an incredibly powerful weapon in the hands of the right writer. Since it is a complex and deeply negative feeling, it can be difficult to portray it accurately, but if you can, your audience is practically guaranteed to sympathize with the shocked character.

This allows you to underscore the traumatic and damaging nature of the scene, buy goodwill for your character, and make your entire story feel more emotionally profound.

Here's an example of a character experiencing shock. Feel free to use it as a model for your own work: Albert trusted his friend to look after his house while he was out of town for the weekend. When he returns home, his friend is nowhere to be found, and his house has been robbed.

Surroundings

961. Albert's whole world was closing in on him, fading to black at the edges.

962. For a long time, Albert just stood in his entranceway, with his mouth hanging open and his hand still gripping the doorknob.

963. Albert knew that he should call the police, or at least start taking an inventory of stolen items, but he couldn't seem to make his legs move; he didn't know where to start.

964. It was as if someone had come in with a wrecking ball and spun it around a million times until everything was reduced to rubble.

965. The neighborhood kids were horsing around outside, making lots of noise, but Albert couldn't even hear them; he was on an entirely different planet.

966. Albert should have been trying to track down his stuff, but instead he spent the night sitting on his couch, staring at the wall where his television used to hang.

967. On opening the door, Albert felt as though he were instantly pushed off a cliff.

Appearance

968. Albert left his mouth gaping open for so long that it felt like it was filled with sandpaper.

969. Albert slowly scanned the chaos that was once his living room with blank, expressionless eyes; the depth of his loss still hadn't registered.

970. Albert felt like his whole face was frozen in place, like he couldn't have smiled or frowned no matter how hard he tried.

971. The vein pulsing wildly in his temple was the only sign that Albert wasn't sleeping standing up.

972. Albert's face looked gaunt and drained; he looked like a shadow of himself.

973. Albert winced and bit his lower lip, unsure of what to do next.

Actions

974. Albert slowly paced around his home, wading through the debris that the robbers left behind.

975. Albert sunk down on his couch and put his head between his knees.

976. Albert felt like he was moving on autopilot as he poured himself a bowl of cereal and ate breakfast in the middle of the disaster zone.

977. Albert wanted to put his fist through the wall--it wasn't as if it would make his house look much worse--but he just couldn't muster up the energy.

978. Albert picked up his phone and called the friend who was supposed to be watching the house; but he hung up before he answered. What could he possibly tell him that Albert didn't already know?

979. Albert thumbed through his record collection in a stupor, perversely irritated that the robbers didn't consider it valuable enough to steal.

980. It was two days before Albert finally called the police. They asked him why he'd waited so long; he told them that the thought had only just occurred to him.

CHAPTER ELEVEN

Emotion Perception

The last key area that we'll break down is by no means the least important: emotion perception. Perception is a process or state of awareness. The more perceptive to emotions someone is, the more likely they are to be aware of their own and other people's feelings and emotions.

Emotion perception by itself isn't an emotion, but, it is important as a vehicle to see and experience a wide range of emotions. Without emotion perception, your characters wouldn't feel anything and that would make for a very mechanical and robotic story!

Characters with strong emotion perception can empathize with others which helps create insightful narratives. You can draw the reader into greater depths of understanding as your character is able to gain insight into the pain, fear and happiness felt by other characters.

On the flip side, characters with a lack of emotion perception, like narcissists, also serve to be interesting characters for your readers. They're the characters that often create conflict and mystery. Historically, such characters have usually been villains—the cold blooded murderers who shock people as they often have no empathy or concern for others.

This final chapter will give you a form of emotion perception that you may be familiar with—sensitivity; and it shows how sensitivity can be used with any of the emotions that we have explored in this book. You can use emotion perception in your writing to give your character's emotions a second dimension; how their feelings are perceived by another character.

Once you've mastered emotion perception, you'll be able to enhance and provide new meaning and insight to all the emotions that we have explored in this book!

Sensitivity

A sensitive character is extremely perceptive of other peoples' emotions, and empathizes with them as well. They can detect minor changes in moods, and are very careful not to insult or irritate anyone. Sensitive characters are experts at putting themselves in other peoples' shoes, and they can lend a voice of tolerance and reason to any situation.

Sensitivity is very subtle, but if it is used correctly, it can become the backbone of a character's personality. It affects every part of their worldview and their actions, which can be quite useful for adding psychological depth, making the character seem more real and well-rounded.

Sensitive characters are great at nurturing their friends and calming down their enemies, and since they are so observant and focused, they are very difficult to fool or confuse. All of these qualities mean that they are uniquely helpful to writers, because they can be used to overcome obstacles and advance the plot.

Below we have an example of sensitivity in action; use it as a template for one of your own characters: Stanley is a university student studying to become a psychologist. He is very sensitive, and now that he's starting to learn some therapy techniques he's become concerned about his roommate Bobby's happiness and fulfillment.

Surroundings

981. Everywhere Stanley looked—in class, walking around downtown, even at the movies—people were unhappy. He could see it in their eyes, he could hear it in their voices.

982. When his friend Bobby snapped at him, Stanley felt his veins go cold; he hated disappointing people, even for a second.

983. Stanley felt like he had superpowers; he could see straight through a complete stranger's defenses and get to the core of whatever was bothering them.

984. Stanley's heart went out to his roommate; he had so many challenges in life, but he still put on a brave face and tried his best.

985. Stanley loved parades; he would feed off of the excitement and happiness that surrounded him.

986. Stanley didn't pester Bobby about his problems; he knew that he would talk to him when he was ready.

987. When Stanley walked into the room, he could instantly tell that something was bothering Bobby.

Appearance

988. As Stanley listened to Bobby talk about his troubles, he frowned slightly and nodded his head.

989. Stanley smiled and wrinkled his nose, glad that his friend was feeling better.

990. Stanley bit his lip and winced, already certain that he'd said the wrong thing.

991. Stanley gave Bobby a sympathetic half smile and shrugged.

992. Stanley wiped a tear from the corner of his eye; he knew that he had to be objective and professional, but the story was so sad that he couldn't help himself.

993. Stanley closed his eyes and shook his head solemnly; he couldn't believe that people could be so cruel.

Actions

994. Stanley wrapped an arm around Bobby's shoulder and told him to look on the bright side.

995. When Bobby snapped at him, Stanley winced as if he'd just been punched in the gut.

996. Stanley laughed extra hard at Bobby's joke; he knew that his friend could use his support now more than ever.

997. Stanley decided to do most of the chores that week; Bobby had enough on his plate already.

998. After Bobby yelled at him, Stanley spent the rest of the night in bed under the covers, trying to forgive himself for acting so ridiculously.

999. Stanley wrote Bobby a long letter offering his friend emotional support in his time of need.

1000. Stanley had a lot of trouble watching sad movies; he would always get so worried about the main characters that he had to leave the room.

CHAPTER TWELVE

Create Impact!

Now that you've got 1000 sample sentences to show a wide ranges of emotions and perceptions, you can use them to create strong impact and make your story memorable.

After all, people don't always remember what you tell them, but they remember how you make them *feel*.

This book is for you and your writing—so that you have exactly what you need to help your reader *feel* what you want them to feel when reading your masterpiece. Whether it be anger, fear, joy, despair, hope etc....

But... most importantly, 'showing' not 'telling' will make your piece communicate on a personal level to your reader. It will make the words on your page *feel* human.

And, that is something very special indeed.

Now, go forth and write that masterpiece of yours.

Printed in Great Britain
· by Amazon

62214074R00090